Find the Fire

"This isn't just a book about how to be motivated and work hard. It's about how to get inspired or, if your inspiration is waning, how to get re-fired so that you can do work that matters."

— David Burkus,
Author, *Under New Management*

"If you've lost that spark at work or want to help someone who has, you face a problem. Most people don't think they can inspire. If you want to understand inspiration so you can do it, Scott Mautz's book will help. He's thought about it deeply, clearly from experience, and explains it so you can understand and practice inspiration more. His key insight that we were inspired at one time points to a simple strategy most people miss: to undo losing it, which is easier and more effective than creating it from scratch. His writing is playful, too; a refreshing change from many overly serious or heavy books."

—Joshua Spodek
Author, *Leadership Step by Step*

FIND
THE
FIRE

SCOTT MAUTZ

FIND THE FIRE

IGNITE YOUR INSPIRATION—
AND MAKE WORK EXCITING AGAIN

HARPERCOLLINS
LEADERSHIP

AN IMPRINT OF HARPERCOLLINS

Find the Fire

© 2018 Scott Mautz

Published by HarperCollins Leadership, an imprint of HarperCollins Focus LLC.

Any internet addresses, phone numbers, or company or product information printed in this book are offered as a resource and are not intended in any way to be or to imply an endorsement by HarperCollins Leadership, nor does HarperCollins Leadership vouch for the existence, content, or services of these sites, phone numbers, companies, or products beyond the life of this book.

Bulk discounts available. For details visit:
www.harpercollinsleadership.com/bulkquotes
Email: customercare@harpercollins.com

ISBN 978-0-8144-3822-0 (HC)
ISBN 978-1-4002-4568-0 (paperback)

CONTENTS

FIND
THE
FIRE

PART I

THE
ANTI-MUSE

1

The Forces That Drain Our Inspiration

YOU KNOW THE feeling.

Your pulse quickens. You can *feel* the energy welling up inside, thrusting everything else to the peripheral. You can sense the power of possibility while your mind races without constraint. You're filled with a sense of excitement and feel compelled to take action. You're ready . . . to . . . go.

No, not gassiness.

Inspiration.

The most powerful, catalyzing programming we have on our internal hard drive. The Holy Grail of enthusiasm.

Its power extends even beyond that of motivation. Motivation is the pragmatic consequence of inspiration; it's that engineer in you that proceeds in a step-by-step fashion with marching orders in hand until it achieves its goal.

Inspiration is a three-beers-in guitar solo. It yields a moment of galvanizing energy and vision that precedes motivation and shoves it into action.

With motivation, we take hold of an idea and run with it.

With inspiration, an idea takes hold of us.

Inspiration's résumé is Navy SEAL impressive. Research has clearly linked it to the enhancement of well-being and the sense that one is living a full life.[1] Inspiration produces moments that fill us and move us, stirring us to our greatest accomplishments. It has built jaw-dropping buildings and torn down oppressive walls. It has woven spellbinding pages, spit in the face of terrorism with heroic acts, pitched the winning bold idea to the conservative client, hit the shot at the buzzer, started a business on a shoestring, taught English in the jungle, burst breathtaking beauty onto a canvas, and finally taken that accounting class.

It's a force that makes things so.

So . . . where has yours gone?

And why isn't it at work for you?

You're not alone—far too many of us no longer feel a sense of inspiration at work. In fact, research shows that *over 70 percent of us* have lost that loving feeling.

The sense of inspiration was always there when you started your career (or even your current job); it was everywhere. Everywhere, that is, before transaction replaced transcendence, and process supplanted possibility. Before your impact started to dwindle and you felt yourself shrinking. Before monotony replaced magic. Before you started working for that boss you'd describe at best as milquetoast or at worst as soul-sucking.

By the way, you won't get much help on that last front, unfortunately.

Research shows that 55 percent of employees cite the ability to inspire as the single most important leadership attribute they want from their boss, and yet *only 11 percent* say their current manager is inspiring.[2] Furthermore, self-awareness on this front ain't exactly sky-high among the leaders themselves. A study showed leaders gave themselves an average score of 7 out of 10 for how inspirational they thought they were, while their employees scored them on this trait at an average of 4 out of 10 *or lower*.[3]

Yup—your boss thinks he's inspirational like in *Good Will Hunting*, while you daydream of hunting for another job.

The scarcity of inspiration is clearly having an impact on us, as another global study reported that *just 12 percent of employees* worldwide feel optimistic at work.[4]

That can't be good.

Research shows that optimism is the single biggest predictor of resiliency and even has the power to undo the negative effects of a stressful experience.[5] So, it's really not something you want to try to do without.

Still another study showed that among leaders receiving the lowest percentile scores for inspirational ability, productivity was dreadful. Some 56 percent of employees working for such bosses negatively self-rated their productivity[6] (but positively self-rated their impulsivity for taking a hammer to their temple).

And when we do manage to eke out some inspiration at work, it's hard to hold onto. Almost 70 percent of us find it hard to stay inspired at work.[7]

The message here is don't wait around for your leaders to inspire you and keep you inspired. Apparently there's a landfill worth of books on "How to be an inspirational leader" still gathering dust on the bedside nightstands of leaders everywhere.

It's time to take the matter into your own hands.

Now, I know that conventional logic tells you that you need to be inspired by external forces—you can't ignite your own pilot light. I know common beliefs and classic historical accounts will tell you that you have to be patient—inspiration is a mysterious, fickle force that will appear when it's good and ready, a force over which you have no control, like David Hasselhoff.

I disagree.

While I will grant you that inspiration can be elusive, it can, in fact, be *codified and coaxed*. You don't have to helplessly wait around for it to happen to you—*you can create the conditions where inspiration is much more likely to occur.*

And I'll show you how.

Frankly, the prevailing wisdom isn't doing a whole lot for us. As the data clearly shows, we aren't exactly prevailing in the "inspired at work" department.

So, let's get on with the art and science of self-inspiring. As the Russian composer Tchaikovsky advised on finding inspiration, "If we wait for the mood, without endeavoring to meet it half-way, we easily become indolent and apathetic."[8]

I'm on a mission to help you reignite your inspiration at work.

Let's find the fire.

THE FIRST SPARK

Self-inspiration is first and foremost, a choice.

Dr. Gerald Bell, a professor at the University of North Carolina, asked 4,000 retired executives, average age of 70, one question: *If you could live your life over again, what would you do differently?*

The number-one response?

I should have understood more about my cell phone plan.

Just kidding. Actually they said *I should have taken charge of my life and set my goals earlier.*[9]

I can't imagine that one of your goals is to feel uninspired in your work life, nor can I imagine such a state makes you feel in charge of your life. You probably don't need 4,000 aging executives who watch too much of the *Golf Channel* to tell you what you already know deep inside—it's time to take charge and make change—and it's up to you.

The first spark is struck in one of three ways:

1. You choose to view your old job in a new light. You see it for the possibilities it yet still contains to reignite your inspiration.

2. You decide, in your heart of hearts, it's time to move on and find new work. But you first commit to understanding the triggers and warning signs of what keeps and drains our inspiration over time so that you can inform your search and know what to look for/ensure absence of at your potential new employer, and make a move that will stick.

3. If you're lucky enough to be in a place where you really do feel inspired in your job, you then choose to elevate your awareness of why that's the case and how to keep it so.

In any scenario, it's time to look closer—much closer—at this supposed mystery called inspiration.

WHAT INSPIRES US?

Let us begin with the basic question, "What inspires us?"

The answer, of course, is as individual as the person answering it (aside from the hugely popular response of "Super Bowl halftime show"). It might be a compelling vision, a specific song, your favorite painting, your boss's boss, or a well-crafted quote. It might be a story of heroism, a talented coworker, a tale of triumph, a particular idea, or a beautiful sunset.

So, when we're feeling uninspired, we can think of what inspires us and try to find ways to incorporate more of it in our life. Makes sense.

Unfortunately, the net effect of our efforts is often too tepid and too temporary—as sobering statistics on our current state of inspiration at work indicate.

We're missing something.

Asking and acting on "What inspires me?" at first glance seems like fertile territory, and yet a fundamental, deep-seated lack of inspiration persists.

To find a more sustaining solution versus temporary spikes, to find common powerful themes to draw from amid a dizzying array of individualized and random sources of fleeting inspiration, you must go further and dig deeper.

THE ANATOMY OF INSPIRATION

Let us begin this excavation with a deeper understanding of inspiration. Leading research on inspiration reveals three defining characteristics:[10]

1. Our inspiration can be *evoked*; we become inspired *by* (a leader, an act of bravery, a sunset, a story of redemption, remarkable work). Responsibility for becoming inspired is ascribed to something beyond the self, something that has engendered a deep appreciation.

2. Our inspiration can come from *within*, triggered when we gain an awareness of better possibilities and when new interests or insights are revealed. This reorients us toward something more imperative than our usual focus (an innovative idea piques our interest, a new challenge stirs us, a renewed relationship reenergizes us, a better way to work becomes evident).

3. Any of these inspirations can *compel us to act*—we have a strong motivation to act on and actualize the idea, interest, or insight and/or express or imitate the qualities expressed in the inspirational stimulus. It is here that we are inspired to work with conviction, joy, excitement, confidence, control, and pride. We're inspired to create, connect, produce, and pursue ideas and interests with vigor.

This last characteristic of inspiration, being compelled to act, is of course the most critical. Many things can inspire us; it's what we decide to *do* with the inspiration that really matters.

If only it were that easy.

Each characteristic contains inherent challenges to unlocking sustained self-inspiration.

The problem with being inspired *by* is that by definition, it's *passive*. It implies involvement of external forces, something more likely to be out of our control, less likely to be reliable, and that you often have to wait for. And the associated inspiration is often fleeting, by the way. Your inspirational CEO can fire you up for only so long before you find yourself back at your desk, trying to put your finger on the funk you're in (and trying to move your finger fast enough on your Fruit Ninja game app).

The difficulty with inspiring from within and gaining awareness of better possibilities, insights, or interests is that it is *elusive*. It's not obvious as to how one goes about revealing such gems. New insights are rare by design; they wouldn't be insightful if they were mere common knowledge. On the surface here, happenstance plays far too big a role.

The issue with feeling compelled to act is that it all too easily gets *repressed*—by our soul-crushing work environment or our own debilitating hang-ups.

So the core elements of inspiration are inherently *passive, elusive,* or *repressed*—which sounds like the name of a teenager's memoir. The point is that this is hardly fodder for believing sustained self-inspiration is right around the corner. No wonder inspiration levels are so alarmingly low in the workplace.

Now that you understand the anatomy of inspiration and the inherent challenges of inspiring oneself, you've hopefully gained an appreciation for why asking and acting on "What inspires me?" simply isn't a robust enough approach. You aren't alone starting with this question, by the way, as research indicates we most frequently ask this of ourselves when we're attempting to get re-grounded and light a spark. While a reasonable starting place, the question tells only half the story.

A BETTER QUESTION

The question to ask yourself, in fact, is not "What inspires me?"

Instead, real insight and application lies in the question, *"How did I lose my inspiration in the first place?"*

Remember, we all had it—we started our jobs filled with inspiration. As I mentioned before, we didn't even have to think about it really—it was just there, everywhere, like half-finished highway construction.

What happened?

How might we return to that blissful time?

When we closely analyze how it is that we tend to lose our inspiration, it reveals root causes lying under the surface that have been slowly draining our inspiration over time. Such causes derail us from all the most critical things that can *self-sustain* inspiration.

Furthermore, such analysis engenders more control because, when known, the root causes are things that *you can do something about*—so inspiration no longer has to seem so passive, elusive, or repressed.

That's why "How did I lose my inspiration in the first place?" is such a powerful question—a question for which the answer, and its implications, will inspire you.

THE MUSE

Before examining this vital question, let me return for just a moment to the related but less potent question of "What inspires us?" The forces behind our inspiration have long been debated and are often shrouded in mystery. In fact, early accounts on the source of our inspiration actually linked it to madness. Socrates labeled inspiration as "a state of manic possession or enthusiasm."[11] Other early interpretations of inspiration attributed it to the unconscious mind, while still others linked it to the supernatural. Still others have linked it to Lionel Richie.

A more universally known explanation comes to us from Greek and Roman mythology. Zeus and Mnemosyne had nine daughters: nine goddesses who each presided over different factions of art and science. Legend goes that these daughters serve as the spirit or source that inspires an artist. You may know the goddesses by their stage name—the Nine Muses. You've probably heard of an artist "waiting for his muse" to gift him with the inspiration required to create and discover. The Nine Muses are so effective at dumping inspiration into the heads of artists that they need their own warehouse for the net output—the "museum." The word *music* also comes from these mythological maidens.

Now, to blow your mind.

What if there were not only such muses at work in the real world, but there were counterforces at work as well? What if there were powerful forces laboring to actually *kill* our inspiration?

There are.

And guess what?

There are nine of them.

These forces aren't goddesses, though. They're fiends.

And they're hell-bent on stripping your work life of inspiration.

They are the Anti-Muses.

THE ANTI-MUSES

I've discovered there are indeed such evil forces at work—but knowledge brings hope. Once you're aware of and understand these inspiration sappers you can address them and foster the conditions that will reignite your inspiration at work—and sustain it. A very specific and holistic how-to exists to overcome each force, and I'll share them all with you.

Let us meet the nine fiends and discover how dousing their efforts can reignite our inspiration.

1. *Fear*—The Anti-Muse of Fear is the most devastating of them all. In her presence our sense of inspiration is all but vanquished. We're in no state of mind to receive inspiration. We can become immobilized, distracted, and thrust into self-doubt mode. Growth and discovery hide in the shadows. Worry replaces wonder.

Inspiration is doomed in the face of three fears in particular: the fear of failure, the fear of change, and the fear of criticism. Chapter 2, "Fear (Relinquished)," will give you the firepower to turn the tables on this arch-enemy of inspiration. Specifically, you'll discover how fear interrupts our ability to get inspired. You'll also learn:

- How to overcome the fear of failure
- How to overcome a fear of change
- How to overcome a fear of criticism

2. *Settling and Boredom*—Most of us have experienced or can imagine a time at work when we have been stuck. Time passes and our drive, interest, and output can wane. We discover we're getting even less than what we know we settled for. Boredom can soon follow. We take lunches that last longer than a jar of VapoRub. Inspiration exits stage left.

The truth is if you know you've settled for too long, or have become bored with your work, you have the power to change it.

The Anti-Muse of Settling and Boredom exists, more than any other such fiend, by our own choice.

So rejecting this force is about choosing to shift to a more open mindset and seek out new experiences. Chapter 3, "Settling and Boredom (Rejected)," will show you how. You'll discover how to shatter a sense of settling and boredom and open the windows of inspiration by learning:

- How to embolden yourself to take more risks
- How to start learning and growing again
- How to make your own opportunities

3. *Inundation*—When we're making things happen, it happens to feel great. More than that, we're inspired to keep going, as we can sense the impact we're having. One Harvard researcher refers to this as the "progress principle"—of all the things that can boost emotions, motivation, perceptions, and levels of inspiration during a workday, the single most important is making *progress*, especially on work that matters to us.[12]

The Anti-Muse of Inundation is the mortal enemy of our ability to make progress at work (second only to jammed copy machines). She interrupts the virtuous cycle of progress that inspires us to keep going, which fuels more progress, which further inspires us, and so on.

In Chapter 4, "Inundation (Relieved)," you'll discover how to quell your sense of inundation and enable progress, in partnership with inspiration, to do its thing. You'll learn:

- How to make choices and set priorities
- How to stop procrastinating and get s#@! done
- How to stop being a perfectionist
- How to master the art of pushback
- How to ask for help and look good doing it

4. *Loss of Control*—Psychology research shows that when we feel we have control over what happens in our lives and can favorably influence outcomes, even in times of duress, we're also much more likely to look within ourselves for inspiration (as opposed to waiting for it to happen to us).[13]

So when we have a sense of control, we'll take more control, even over such a "divine" force as inspiration. We're less distracted, are less likely to feel victimized, and feel much more able to take note of and act on inspiring cues all around us. Chapter 5, "Loss of Control (Reverted)," will teach you how to revive inspiration by taking control back from this whirlwind Anti-Muse. Specifically, you'll learn:

- How you give away your power
- How you can take back a sense of power
- How you emit power

5. *Dwindling Self-Belief*—Inspiration is a profoundly strong force that in turn requires a base level of inner strength from which to draw—like a tornado needs the atmospheric conditions of a thunderstorm to form and then unleash its fury. This inner fortitude takes the form of an engaged, optimistic, able, self-confident presence. Research bears this out, indicating that inspired people report substantially higher levels of important psychological resources, including belief in their own abilities, self-esteem, and optimism.[14] Plus they're more likely to wear their skinny jeans on casual Friday.

When such a presence becomes a mere shadow of itself, ground to a pulp in the daily grind, our impact and sense of inspiration evaporate. Without a revitalization of our personal presence, we begin to withdraw from our job more and more. We unwittingly shut ourselves out from passion and possibility until eventually the siren song of inspiration is doomed to fall on deaf ears.

Chapter 6, "Dwindling Self-Belief (Revitalized)," will help you rebound against this Anti-Muse by reinvigorating your self-belief. You will thus maximize your receptivity and readiness for inspiration. You'll learn:

- How to elevate your self-confidence
- How to persevere in the face of challenges

- How to be mindfully present
- How to earn respect

6. *Disconnectedness*—Psychology professor and inspiration expert Tobin Hart asked research respondents to describe the opposite, or the lack of, inspiration. The most common response (after "the Department of Motor Vehicles") was: "I experience a lack of connection. I feel isolated and alone."[15] It probably isn't surprising to learn that research shows we become immensely uninspired when we become disconnected from those we are surrounded by each day at work. These human connections are deep wells of energy from which inspiration can take form.

Chapter 7, "Disconnectedness (Reversed)," will detail how to reverse the net effect of the Anti-Muse of Disconnectedness. You'll learn how to:

- Reconnect with coworkers and reenergize interactions by learning how to go beyond mere collaboration to camaraderie
- Do so while still cultivating the healthy debate necessary for producing inspiring ideas

7. *Dearth of Creating*—Countless studies and raw common sense will tell you that creativity blossoms when the artist, musician, employee, etc. becomes inspired. The link between inspiration and creativity is irrefutable—the former spurs the latter.

But is the inverse true?

Does the act of being creative inspire you?

Chapter 8, "Dearth of Creating (Reconstituted)," will prove this an emphatic yes and underscore the travesty at hand when we find that we've somehow stopped creating. The Dearth of Creating Anti-Muse is doing its stifling deed when we find that we've stopped expressing ourselves through our work and producing unique output that we're proud to share with the world.

Let what you're capable of making/producing/writing/performing/leading come bursting forth. Make this Anti-Muse cower with the furious roar of your creative voice being heard once again. In Chapter 8, learn:

- A powerful, detailed method for unleashing your creativity

8. Insignificance—A close second to Fear for her dastardly skill at thoroughly suppressing a sense of inspiration is Insignificance, the most deep-seated of the Anti-Muses. She materializes as a feeling that what we're spending our precious time on isn't making a difference on anything that matters to us, and that we don't really matter, or simply don't measure up to others.

When we can bring a sense of significance and meaning back to what we're doing, we work with a hum, an almost palpable vibrating energy that replaces the numbness we felt beforehand. This energy drives us to advance our pursuits and jars our mind open to discover new worthy pursuits, all of which attracts more such energy—in the form of inspiration.

So how, then, do we spend less time on the indent of someone else's footprint and get to work on our own? How do we bring back a sense of importance to our efforts? (Besides suddenly and weirdly asking coworkers to add the title "Dr." when addressing us)

Chapter 9, "Insignificance (Reformulated)," will address these questions and share prompts and/or mantras for leaving your mark—time-tested manners through which you can have an impact. And impact invites inspiration.

9. Lack of Evocation—In the opening of this chapter I pleaded that you not rely on external forces to evoke a sense of inspiration, and instead look within and attack the draining counterforces. That said, I want to leave no stone unturned in this vital pursuit.

But this Anti-Muse, Lack of Evocation, is a tricky foe as she's the most patient evil-doer of the bunch.

She will wait forever, hoping that you'll wait forever.

And the longer you passively wait for inspiration to appear, the stronger its cumulative negative effect (like that of reality television). More specifically, when inspiration isn't evoked after a sustained period, your belief that it will ever show up rapidly wanes. You begin to mentally write off your job as hopeless and may even miss signals of inspiration trying to break through along the way—a double whammy.

You deserve an occasional window of evoked inspiration to go along with the doors of inspirational opportunities you're about to open elsewhere.

To enable this, proactivity, not passivity, is the way forward. Hunting for external stimulus likely to spur inspiration simply requires knowing where to look. Chapter 10, "Lack of Evocation (Rediscovered)," will teach you:

- How to evoke inspiration from external sources, including understanding the conditions and behaviors that do so
- How to convert an inspiration-draining boss into an inspiration-evoking one

So there you have it—it was my absolute displeasure to introduce you to the Anti-Muses—the nine fiends that drain our inspiration. Fortunately, I was also able to provide an overview for each strain of Antidote you'll be learning much more about in subsequent chapters. (In Chapter 11, "The Bonfire," you'll also be given a plan for putting all the tools in this book to work for you in an organized and intentional manner to ensure that the fire of inspiration is fully rekindled.)

Let us now proceed with concocting and then administering each Antidote.

And let's do so with haste. Time is precious and everyone knows that the only way to immortality is to put a man in charge of remembering birthdays.

Inspiration, you're more than on the mend—you're about to be wholly reignited.

PART II

THE ANTIDOTE

2

Fear

(RELINQUISHED)

EXACTLY 543.7 MILES.

The distance from Sydney, Australia, to Melbourne is dread inducing enough even to the heartiest of ultra-marathoners—and that's before you throw in the fact that challenging hills populate the expanse.

Hailed by many as "The World's Most Grueling Athletic Competition," the Westfield Run is not for the faint of heart, to say the least. On a scale of 1 to 10 for difficulty, this challenge measures "sadist." One can only imagine the level of athletic prowess and preparation required to compete in such a horrifically grueling event.

So on race day, April 27, 1983, it wasn't surprising to see a supremely fit-looking group of entrants at the registration table, all decked out in the latest running shoe technology and garb emblazoned with corporate sponsorship from the likes of Nike and Adidas. Each runner was a world class athlete who had been specifically training for this event; the best of the best ultra-marathoners, twenty-somethings with something to prove to the world, and themselves.

Not surprisingly, no one paid attention to Cliff Young when he nudged his way up to the tent to get his race number, dressed in holey overalls and rubber rain boots. In fact, he passed as a spectator, until he joined the other runners as they congregated at the race's start point. Suddenly, many did take notice.

Surely, this toothless, bedraggled man wasn't actually going to run? The media approached him, thinking it was a publicity stunt of some sort. Turns out it wasn't. The scrawny potato and sheep farmer fully intended to race. He told the press he'd finish the race (which very few did) because he was used to corralling, by foot, over 2,000 sheep on a 2,000-acre farm when storms rolled in—a duty necessitated by the fact that his family was too poor to afford a horse or tractor. As he told the press that day: "Sometimes I would have to run those sheep for two or three days. It took a long time, but I'd catch them. I believe I can run this race."

Bold statement considering the fact that I don't think I could *drive* this race without keeling over from exhaustion.

Befuddled, the press and onlookers watched with amusement as the race began. It appeared everyone's skepticism was correct; during the opening day of the race the farmer soon fell dramatically and hopelessly behind the pack, he and his rain boots quickly tens of miles behind the other runners. He drew further cackles with his gait, which was much more of an awkward foot-beside-foot shuffle than it was the loping stride of a seasoned marathoner.

He didn't run like Forrest Gump, but comically had gumption to spare.

Five days, fifteen hours, and four minutes later, however, no one was laughing.

By then, Cliff Young, the easy target for ridicule that he was, had won the Westfield Run, finishing more than ten hours ahead of the other runners and obliterating the previous record *by more than two days.*

Oh, and one other thing—he was 61 years old.

You see, no one told Cliff that ultra-marathoners ran for eighteen hours, then slept for six. What did he know? That first night, after a brief nap of about an hour he simply got up and kept going. No preconceived notions of how it was supposed to be done or what's been proven to work, no master stroke of running strategy, no fine-tuned world beating running technique—just keep running while the others slept.

The other runners woke up to find out Cliff Young was now miles and miles ahead of them, shuffling slowly along in a modern day tortoise and hare affair. And so it went for over five and a half days, with the other runners never so much as catching a whiff of Cliff after that first night.[1]

Cliff Young was deeply inspired to run such a ludicrous distance because, in his own words: "I like to finish what I start doing. I like to see it through to the end, to the best of my ability."[2] And what better challenge than to try to finish something that so few others ever could or have.

The secret to Cliff's success, you ask?

No, not steroids. At least I don't think.

Young's inspiration to start and finish such a herculean feat was *never, not even for a moment, dampened by fear*—although it had every opportunity to be.

He knew not of the fear of failure—which could have understandably paralyzed him in the face of such an audacious undertaking. He just ran. He didn't have preexisting norms and self-doubt born from comparing himself to others crippling him from the get-go. In fact, when all was said and done, he pushed the five other finishers of the race to their own individual successes, with each one breaking the previous Westfield record in their attempt to catch Cliff. To honor their success, Cliff actually gave away much of the $10,000 winner's pot to the other five finishers, citing that they were tougher then he was. He didn't even know there was a prize for winning—stating again as he gave away the money, and thus further endearing himself to Australia, that he was inspired to just "finish what he started."

He certainly could have succumbed to the fear of criticism—he wasn't ignorant of the laughs and looks he got as he started the race (the same sort I get when I try to grow a beard). On that first day, the press and a nation of onlookers now joining in and compelled by his story, feared for Cliff's life, certain that the old man would collapse and die at the end of the first day of such exertion. Calls came in from around the continent of Australia as the race wore on, begging race officials to make Cliff stop. Those concerns were shared with Cliff along the way. But still Cliff ran, impervious to the critics, the doubts, and the fears of all.

After Cliff's win, life changed at a blurring and uncomfortable pace for the simple farmer. But he did not bend to the fear of change. He answered the call to serve as a national hero, the furthest thing possible from being a potato and sheep farmer and the last thing on his mind.

And so, still, he ran.

All the way up to eighteen years after his Westfield win, at the age of 79, he ran—this time deeply inspired by his desire to raise money to help homeless children.

Today, the odd style of running Cliff made famous is called the "Young Shuffle" and has been adopted by ultra-marathoners around the world and hailed as a more energy-efficient means of running great lengths. Three winners of the Westfield since Cliff Young have employed the method. And taking in the absolute bare minimum amount of sleep during the race has become standard practice (among ultra-marathoners *and* new parents). More important, Cliff Young inspired an entire country along the way and to this day is hailed as a true Australian legend.[3] Probably bigger than Crocodile Dundee. OK, I have no way of proving that.

Anyway, all this because a country bumpkin refused to let fear, in any form, dampen his inspiration for doing something that mattered to him.

We all have some of the Cliff Young spirit in us—that stoic force bathed in innocence that draws from inspiration for energy and that treats fear as a nonentity. It's a part of us well worth enlisting in the battle, as the Anti-Muse called Fear is insatiable in her need to devour our sense of inspiration and wonder.

THE FEAR EFFECT

Fear will never, ever, stop if left unchecked.

The impact that fear has on inspiration is unquestionably both manifold and malevolent. In general, the negative emotion and energy of fear alters our capacity to harness the positive energy of inspiration. While inspiration presses us forward, fear holds us back.

More specifically, fear assaults our sense of inspiration in five ways:

1. *Fear disrupts the preparedness of our mind for being inspired.* It greatly compromises our ability to focus, be present, still our minds, listen, and reflect—all the necessary state of mind ingredients for being maximally receptive to the advances of inspiration.[4]
2. *Fear blocks action.* If we can work around fear to be inspired *by* something, it then engages in a second stage of interference, keeping us from being inspired *to*. As organizational behavior expert Kevin Cavanagh articulates, "Individuals who do not feel psychologically safe (are experiencing fear) in their work environment may still be inspired by the work they are doing, but feel unsafe in taking the risks to act out being inspired to do something." [5] Neuro-economist Gregory Berns (how bad-ass is that, *neuro-economist*) brings it right down to our brain functions: "The most concrete thing that neuroscience tells us is that when the fear system of the

brain is active, exploratory activity and risk-taking are turned off. Fear prompts retreat" (the opposite of progress).[6]

3. *Fear dissuades discovery and growth.* It creates a stasis that prevents us from discovering new ideas, uncovering new interests, and engaging in things that might bring improvements to our life—all fundamental sources of inspiration.

4. *Fear engages our brain in the wrong conversation.* Instead of encouraging the imagination of inspiring possibilities it narrows our scope of thinking and steers us toward an obsession with limitations and negative thoughts.

5. *Fear distorts reality* and unfairly creates inaccurate, unfounded, but self-accepted truths that further stifle our receptivity to inspiration.

Fear is a formidable enough foe of inspiration—and resultant creativity—that two prominent authors, Elizabeth Gilbert (*Eat, Pray, Love*) and Steven Pressfield (*War of Art*) have personified it in an attempt to keep it at bay. Gilbert likens it to someone who goes along on a car ride with you while you're trying to create. Fear can sit there quietly, but can't touch the radio and most certainly can't drive.[7] Pressfield calls the force that keeps us from progressing our creative endeavors "Resistance," a force (like procrastination or a blockage of disciplined effort) that draws its power from our fear of it.[8] This force snuffs out any wisp of inspiration.

The good news here is you don't need to go so far as to put a face to your fear. You just need to face it down—and stop letting fear limit you.

It's time to tear the bubble wrap off your life.

There is simply too much at stake to stay cocooned. When we press past our fears and venture forth "unprotected," we discover. We set new limits. We imagine. We feel our strengths strengthening and our self-doubts dashed. We learn we can take a punch, and are better for it. We see opportunities, not opposition.

We become inspired once again.

Let's relinquish the hold that fear can have on us by attacking its most debilitating incarnations—the same ones Cliff Young faced down—a Fear of Failure, a Fear of Change, and a Fear of Criticism. These fears must no longer cause us to neglect the astonishment of inspiration.

FEAR OF FAILURE

What are CEOs afraid of more than anything else?

No, not being on *60 Minutes.*

I should first acknowledge, by the way, that we don't typically associate the word *fear* in any context with such titans of industry. After all, as the logic goes, they didn't get to where they are by being afraid of much of anything.

But the truth is, despite breathing such rarified air, they choke on the same thing that we all do—the fear of failure.

The fear of failure is the first of the three most debilitating, inspiration-killing, incarnations of fear that we'll attack.

A *Harvard Business Review* study found this fear to be so common among the corporate elite, in fact, that there's actually a name for it—the "impostor syndrome"—or the fear of being found an incompetent failure. Perhaps this is understandable given that failure by a CEO can have devastating consequences such as job cuts, a plummeting stock price, or a sea of disillusioned employees.

But the problem is that this particular fear can manifest into the realization of the very thing leaders are afraid of. Research shows that a fear of failure at the CEO level cascades down into other dysfunctional behaviors such as a lack of honest conversations, excessive politics, thinking in silos, and a lack of ownership and follow-through.[9]

As for the rest of us, we fare no better on this front. Research indicates that our fear of failure tops the list of our phobias with nearly one in three people having a fear of failure (31 percent), ahead of our fear of public speaking or fear of spiders (30 percent each) or even our fear of the paranormal (15 percent). A close fifth was our fear of another *Transformers* movie being made.

Furthermore, nearly half of all adults (49 percent) admitted that fear of failure "was the biggest roadblock to either not achieving their goals at all, or discouraged them from revisiting their goals."[10]

These are consequences arguably more painful than even those induced by CEOs with such a fear.

And it gets worse.

Imagine a funnel, wide at the top then narrowing to its thin spout at the bottom, like that pictured in Figure 2-1.

FIGURE 2-1
THE FEAR OF FAILURE FUNNEL

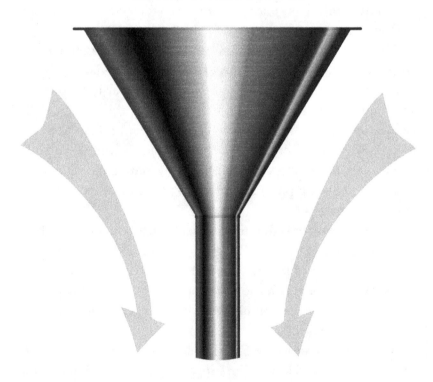

We start out at the top of that funnel with big, wide-open thinking and a huge scope of possibility. Slowly, as we grow more fearful of failure, the width of the funnel contracts. Our thinking becomes narrowed, our perception of possibilities shrinks in diameter. Down and down the funnel we spiral until we find ourselves in a vastly constricted worldview—the narrow spout at the bottom.

This is the Fear of Failure Funnel.

It's where inspiration goes to die.

But we can reverse the flow of this funnel, loosening the binding grip of fear and opening back up grand, imaginative thinking and possibility. We can work our way back up the funnel, wider, slowly wider, toward the invitingly big, open starting point, as we push back against our fear of failure.

And I can show you how.

It comes down to critical *framing*.

When we can bravely and boldly employ the proper Frame of Mind, Frame of Reference, and Frame of Action, we can reverse the inspiration-killing constriction caused by our fear of failure.

Frame of Mind

Stanford psychologist Kelly McGonigal says that studies show people who are considered successful usually don't encounter fewer setbacks than people who aren't considered successful. The critical difference comes from how those setbacks are viewed.[11]

That gets right to the essence of why viewing failure with the right frame of mind is so important.

Here are six powerful ways to reframe how you think of failure; each one can chase away the fear and invite inspiration back in.

1. *There are only three ways to actually fail*—when we quit, when we don't improve, or when we never try.
2. *Failure is an event, not a person*—And never over-generalize that these one-time occasions are indicative of your

trademark imprint or are harbingers of future, wide-spread failure.

3. *Failure doesn't happen* to *you, it happens* for *you*—Tony Robbins once said this of life, but I've also found it to be incredibly true about failure. You need to believe that when you fail, it was for a reason. Perhaps it was so you could experience a sweeter tasting success later on. Or it may have needed to happen so you could learn something vital that would propel you to success. As such, failure is a delay, not a detour. Within this context know that there are two points, literally, to failure: each failure is a temporary point in time, and each failure has a more permanent, positive point to it.

4. *You don't suffer when you fail, your ego does*—And our ego is but one small part of us—albeit the loudest, whiniest, most demanding portion that needs to be knocked down a notch anyway.[12] Despite our best efforts to keep it in check, our ego demands to be fed. But you must remember all the parts of us that are nourished in events of failure. Isolate your ego from your true self when you feel you've failed. Make your ego sit at the kids' table where it belongs while the rest of the adult in you gets on with an enjoyable meal of discovery and growth.

5. *Your fear of failure shouldn't scare you; it's trying to tell you something's worth it*—You wouldn't fear failing at something inconsequential, right? (Other than trying to solve Rubik's Cube at a party, of course—I've never even gotten one side all the same color.)

6. *Failure is a key part of your portfolio*—Netscape founder Marc Andreessen compares a well-managed career to a diversified portfolio. The ideal career contains a wide range of job opportunities, including risky ones ripe with adventure, experimentation, and, yes, even failure. The net of these experiences combines to form a career with a high potential for growth.[13]

It's no different with the range of failures and successes we experience in our life. There is no truly successful person who doesn't have failure as part of their life portfolio.

Although Kanye West would probably beg to differ.

Frame of Reference

As we spiral down the fear of failure funnel, our point of reference narrows. The fear feeds on itself, causing us to infer more and more from a more limited, and misplaced, set of stimuli. Self-fulfilling prophecies become more of a possibility than self-fulfillment.

We reverse this downward spiral when we anchor our frame of reference to something that provides a helpful broadening perspective. What follows are ways to do just that.

- *Slay the Comparison Dragon*—I was conducting research with social media–savvy moms and unexpectedly wakened a beast. A host of moms told me about the extent to which they depended on social media tools like Facebook and Instagram to assist them in their motherly duties. They raved about how they couldn't live without such informative tools and how accessing such tools often served as their only relaxing respite from their harried days.

  Then the phenomenon of what I call "digital mom guilt" slowly revealed itself.

  On the other side of their expressed love for such tools came guilt: guilt because in some cases they were spending as many as ten hours a day on their mobile smartphones, tablets, or laptops. And guilt from the fact that they felt increasingly unworthy relative to the virtual world to which they were increasingly overexposed. Self-congratulatory post after post, perfect picture after perfect picture of people living a life they couldn't—it was all starting to take a toll. Their self-esteem was suffering and they had a growing fear that they were failing to live a good enough life.

The Comparison Dragon had reared its ugly head, as it does with all of us, interrupting everything from our digital daydreaming to our daily lives.

The ironic thing is that this Dragon draws its very power from those it preys upon. The more we compare ourselves to others, the bigger the Dragon gets, striking fear into our hearts with increasing ferocity. We soon feel hopelessly inadequate and are thus moved to inertia. We find ourselves subject to someone else's expectations. We lose sight of *our* definition of success. We find it more and more difficult to exonerate ourselves from what we think others might be thinking.

It's bad enough that we're constantly comparing ourselves to others, but we're not even making fair comparisons, at that. Case in point: To this day I still don't understand why Justin Timberlake insists on comparing himself to me. Poor guy.

Anyway, Kelly Azevedo, founder of She's Got Systems, a productivity jump-starter for entrepreneurs, says what research supports, "We tend to compare our own blooper reel to everyone else's highlights reel."[14]

You know what you have to do.

Like the stoic, lone warrior perched high above the town in the church tower, waiting for the approach of the great winged beast, you must be the one who slays the Comparison Dragon. Put an arrow through its heart and then compare yourself only to what matters—in *your* heart.

- *Take comfort in famous failures*—OK, wait, there is actually one other comparison that is worthy. When we find that even massively successful people have failed along the way, and more than recovered, it's reassuring and inspiring (we're sick like that). It's a universal truth that we fear things a bit less when we know that we're not alone in facing that fear. There is quiet comfort in numbers. Especially when your failures keep company with the likes of the success stories that follow. Ask yourself, "What if these people had let their failure shut them down?"

- The greatest basketball player of all time, Michael Jordan, was cut from his high school team.
- Walt Disney was fired from his job at a newspaper early in his career—they said he lacked imagination.
- Steven Spielberg was rejected from film school three times.[15]
- John Grisham's first book, *A Time to Kill,* was originally rejected twenty-eight times.[16]
- Albert Einstein had the label "mentally slow" put on his permanent school record.[17]
- Henry Ford's first two automobile companies failed.[18]
- Oprah Winfrey was fired from an early job as a television news anchor.[19]
- Jerry Seinfeld was booed off stage in his first stand-up comedy appearance.
- Sir James Dyson suffered through 5,126 failed prototypes before he landed on the first working Dyson vacuum.[20]
- Elvis Presley was fired from the Grand Ole Opry and was told to go back to truck driving.[21]

Feel better? You should. We've *all* been there. It's all in your frame of reference and determination to keep moving forward, which is in your control.

- *Keep the glory of the goal in front of you, but the process at your side*—When you've ventured forth with a risk, stop and remember the potential rewards in the risk/reward equation that you calculated before proceeding. Draw from the thought of achieving those rewards to give you bursts of vitality as you press forward.

  Along the way, however, stay focused on the process of what you're trying to accomplish. Break down your ultimate goal into individual steps or tasks to keep your mind focused and to avoid obsessing over whether or not failure is imminent. Take comfort and pride in the effort, progress, and lessons learned as part of the process.

- *Ask, "What am I really afraid of?"*—Our fear of failure can take on a big, oversized, life of its own. It's important to step back when this fear seems to be looming largest and examine what's really going on. Psychologist Guy Winch says our fear of failure is not the real issue; our fear of shame is the underlying culprit. This is particularly problematic because, as Winch says, "Shame is a psychologically toxic emotion because instead of feeling bad about our actions (*guilt*) or our efforts (*regret*), shame makes us feel bad about who we *are.*"

  Having taken a walk of shame or two in college, I can vouch for that.

  Anyway, in response to this, Winch advises that you need to acknowledge and accept that with failure comes fear *and* shame. Once you do so, you can express these feelings to others and get support and vital reassurance to bolster your self-esteem.[22]

  Darren Hardy, best-selling author and former publisher of *SUCCESS Magazine*, told me that what we really fear is the fear—not the action itself. It's that anticipation leading up to the thing that we're afraid of that kills us. It's why he says you really need only about twenty seconds of courage at a time—the time it takes to plow through the starting point of what you're afraid of doing. He cited research that says our heart rate decreases after actually starting the thing we were afraid of doing (unless that thing is watching the psychedelic boat trip scene from *Willy Wonka*).

Hypnotherapist Tellman Knudson believes we don't actually have a fear of failure per se; we have a fear of failing the first time we try something. This is a deeply ingrained fear we learned from our early school days. Tellman says, "Getting the 'right' answer the first time is the only thing that is rewarded in most schools. Getting the wrong answer is punished in a variety of ways: low grades, scolding and contempt from teachers and peers." This deeply embedded fear can ultimately keep us from ever trying to accomplish anything.[23]

The standard of expecting to get it right the first time is, of course, an unreasonable one—unless you throw knives at magicians' assistants for a living. Most everyone requires practice and a few failed attempts to get it right. In fact, Thomas Watson Sr. of IBM once said, "If you want to increase your success rate, double your failure rate."[24] And yet we hold ourselves to a standard of "first time's the charm" because we've subconsciously come to fear the alternative. Knudson says the solution is to retrain your brain to get out of its comfort zone and try new things. Take a surfing, painting, or archery class—whatever. Get used to failing (and you will if you've never tried it before), and viewing it as a process.[25] And remember, as podcaster Tripp Lanier says, "It's OK to suck."[26]

The point here is to boil down the oversized fear of failure to its true root cause. Then you can attack the more manageable and tangible pieces, seeing them as concrete and more specific challenges you can take on.[27]

- *Reexamine past failures*—Reexamining past failures provides an excellent frame of reference that can make us braver in the future. Odds are we'll recall that we recovered, and were better for it when all was said and done. But we tend to forget that and focus solely on the "in-process" pain of failure.

You'll likely also find that, in retrospect, you were never victimized by failure—a set of specific conditions or circumstances led to the failure. (For me, it has always had something to do with the vernal equinox. Or wind conditions. Sun might have been in my eyes too.)

Right, so, if failure didn't actually kill you, you're victorious, not a victim.

- *Would you rather have regrets?*—This simple, but powerful, frame of reference pits the fear of failing versus never trying and having to live with regrets. The temporary nature of potential failure pales in comparison to the permanent impact of regrets. Keep this tension top of mind to help you buckle down and plow forward through fear. Especially when you don't like the answer to the question, "What happens if I don't act?"
- *Ponder, but only ponder, the worst-case scenario*—Start with the worst thing that could happen, then work back from there as the extremes we concoct rarely happen in the real world (other than the aftermath of holiday family gatherings). More than likely even the actual worst-case scenario itself is manageable once you break it down.

Frame of Action

> "Any motion whatsoever beats inertia,
> because inspiration will always be drawn to motion."
>
> ELIZABETH GILBERT[28]

This element of reversing the funnel is about *specific actions* you can take to steamroll your fear of failure. The idea is to ensure that the energy you spend trying to avoid failure pales in comparison to the energy you spend trying to succeed.

Get going on what follows to move past what's holding you back.

- *Practice getting it wrong*—I mentioned earlier that one of people's greatest fears is public speaking. Interestingly enough, research shows that when someone with this fear is required to practice it, no matter how intense their level of fear, they will eventually become good at it and lose their fear altogether. We all have the ability to reprogram our fears by putting ourselves in situations where we are forced to face them over and over again—until the fear response simply dissipates.[29]

  Our nerve serves us well in this, but so does our neuroplasticity—our brain's well-documented ability to learn and adapt to that which it encounters and conquers over and over.[30]

  So the bottom line is you simply need to get comfortable with being uncomfortable (which describes how I feel in an Abercrombie & Fitch store). Put yourself in situations where you're forced to practice getting it wrong and experiencing just a bit of the very failure you're afraid of. Accept and embrace the mistakes you'll be making along the way, and you'll soon enough see that fear is in the rearview mirror and inspiration is straight ahead.

- *Burn the boats*—When sea-bound Greek armies landed on the shores of their enemies, the first thing they did before preparing for battle was to burn their boats. Suddenly, there was no turning back. You could either press forward to victory or retreat back and drown in the seas of your fear.

  You want to get over your fear of failure and be able to invite inspiration back in?

  Really commit—perhaps even with a bit of dramatic flair, if that's what it takes. Sign up for open mic night before you've written the first word of your stand-up routine. Agree to that intimidating project before you've had one ounce of training. Enroll yourself in a recital before you've learned your first note. Agree to pay for your spouse's Pilates class before you see how hot the instructor is. (Wait, I lost the plot a bit on that last one.)

The point is, even if it's not as dramatic as any of these, making a commitment puts your fear to work for you. Fear of failure disappears when you realize it can't save you.[31]

- *Don't just visualize, actualize*—The bookstore shelves are stuffed with self-help gurus telling you to visualize success. But these books tell you only half the story. Research shows that the positive fantasies and visualizations that people conjure about their future *may actually deplete their energy to pursue them.* You might construct lots of visions about successful outcomes to new endeavors, but when you don't take action on them, they accumulate and soon feel exhausting and overwhelming. So while visualizing success is an important step toward overcoming a fear of failure, you must also take action.[32] As our chapter opening hero, Cliff Young, put it when asked about his race plan: "I reckon you have to keep your joints moving. No matter what you do, you have to keep moving. If you don't wear out, you rust out, and you rust out quicker than you wear out."[33]

  Relatedly, just visualizing success in a sort of daydream fashion, without visualizing the idea of encountering, acting in the face of, and overcoming obstacles, is about as effective as never actually taking action. A study from the *Journal of Experimental Social Psychology* detailed two separate groups of college students—one group was asked to visualize a very positive week ahead of them. The other group was asked to more pragmatically write down any thoughts about the week that might come to mind—good things, unpleasant things they'd have to deal with, all of it. The group that got to live in la-la land reported feeling less energized and actually ended up accomplishing less than the other group. The study showed the importance of maintaining a balance of positive visualization as well as a more practical, imagined actualization that deals with ups and downs.[34]

You can do the same. Picture the bliss of success along with the effort involved in overcoming obstacles along the way—then make it so.

- *Beat fear of the unknown by knowing more*—Our fear of failure is underscored by what we don't know and thus speculate and spiral downward upon. It stands to reason that if you know more, the acreage of unknown is less— thus your fear is diminished.

    Ask yourself if you've truly done your homework before embarking on something you're afraid to fail at. Build on small steps of progress and knowledge gained along the way, slowly but surely reducing the radius of the unknown. Expand your knowledge and level of clarity on what it really takes to succeed in your planned endeavor.

    It's also vital to have a well thought through contingency plan you can put into play should things go awry. Think through how you'll handle actual failure and how long it might take you to recover. And no, binge-watching *Game of Thrones* while scarfing down Ho-Ho's and pizza is not a *Find the Fire* sanctioned recovery plan.

    The truth is that while confident people are quite certain they will succeed, they are just as certain in how they will handle failure. The bottom line here is to lessen your mindless fear of failure by turning your endeavor into an intellectual pursuit—before you even get started.

- *Expose and expel your anxieties*—Our subconscious self reminds us all day long of our anxieties, firing off little self-doubting statements without us even realizing it. "That won't work," "You'll end up looking dumb," "People will think you don't know what you're doing," "Oh my God, did I have something in my teeth that whole time?!"

Anyway, so goes the fear of failure whisperer.

Soon, these subtle self-doubts become very real self-limitations. But you can expose those anxieties and keep them from doing their evil work by being aware and on high alert when it's happening, and then refusing to listen. Just let this internal chatter pass right through you, like when you're flipping through inane radio talk shows until you land on a channel you like.

Computer programmer Paul Ford took it a step further when he created AnxietyBox—a service in which you confess your anxieties and then receive emails from your anxiety, all day long. Your in-box fills with messages like "Your whole life you've just been incapable and boring" or "It's hard to be a leader when you're awful" and "It's true that you are basically faux-intelligent."[35] You soon realize just how ridiculous and damaging your inner chatter can be, and you can then cathartically delete each and every malevolent self-message.

You certainly don't have to go as far as signing up for this service; the key here is to not let the anxieties behind your fear of failure subtly spam your mind. You can externalize and expel them.

FEAR OF CHANGE

The fear of change is the second of the three most debilitating incarnations of fear to be addressed.

An escalating amount of neuroscience research increasingly indicates that change is tough on us. Our brains are wired to value longevity.

One study showed that people who viewed a painting they were told was done in 1905 found it much more aesthetically pleasing than the group who were told the same painting was done in 2005. Another study found that people were much more favorably predisposed toward acupuncture when told it had been around for 2,000 years than the group who were told it was around for 250 years.[36]

We like that which has been around a while and so are predisposed to fear the new.

Change also disrupts the efficient habits that our brain locks onto to conserve energy. When faced with change, the prefrontal cortex works supremely hard to process new ideas and patterns—which can be exhausting as the brain already uses 25 percent of our energy.[37] (The other 75 percent is drained by slow coffee baristas.)

Change threatens our sense of stability and robs us of our sense of control. When we're unsure whether the change means we'll still have a job, or if we'll hate our new boss, or if we'll be working in a winning environment anymore, it's hard to focus on much else.

We also fear change because we fear that we might lose what's associated with that change. Our aversion to loss can cause logic to fly out the window. This is why research shows that gamblers at a horse track who are having a losing day are most likely to bet the long shots, at terrible odds, on the last race of the day.[38] They're faced with the realization of loss and are willing to bet on a horse with 20:1 odds, a bet they'd never walk in thinking they'd make—all because of our natural and violent aversion to loss.

How can a sense of inspiration peak through all these dark clouds?

By following what follows.

Nine Ways to Negate the Fear of Change

1. *Turn resistance into resolution.* I know you know this, but change will happen. But what you may not fully realize are the times when you're unfairly resisting change; it's important to be self-aware on this front. If you need extra incentive besides the fact that fear of change blocks growth and opportunity, which

in turn keeps inspiration at bay, know this—a study has shown that exhibiting fear of change is one of the most career-limiting moves you can make.[39] (Right up there with using your corporate card to buy Pokémon power-ups.)

You have to let go of how great things used to be, stop seeking out others who think like you in an effort to form an anti-change support group, and simply resolve to accept uncertainty.

I recognize how difficult this last one can be—popular podcaster Tim Ferriss once said, "People will choose unhappiness over uncertainty."[40] And once again, neuroscience doesn't help us either. Research shows that uncertainty registers in our brain much like an error does—it needs to be corrected before we can feel comfortable again. We crave certainty because it fixes this error. When we don't have certainty it burns extra neural energy, which can undermine our performance and cause us to disengage from the here-and-now.[41]

But accept uncertainty you must, and then move quickly to resolving to change. Stanford's McGonigal references our New Year's resolutions to confirm what you intuitively know already, that "when people resolve to change, they immediately feel more confident, in control, and hopeful."[42] All of which are potential antecedents to inspiration.

2. *Believe that you have the competence for change.* We often get apprehensive about change because we imagine it will leave us exposed as incapable of handling its outcome. Instead, insist to your doubting self that you have the competence (or can get it if needed) to succeed on the other side of change. You've shown this to be true before, right? For example, think of the times when you took on a new role or started working with a new technology. Perhaps you were apprehensive at first but soon enough, with a little training, practice, trial and error, and application of your ability (and maybe even actually reading the directions—*gentlemen*), you found yourself getting along just fine. We tend to forget these little victories and instead imagine defeat.

3. *Think of change like a software upgrade.*[43] Change can yield You 2.0—a better version of yourself. The key is to move from thinking "beware" to thinking "benefit" when faced with change. That's because in truth, change is one of the most powerful professional development catalysts in existence. So download and upgrade.

4. *Find your anchor.* We hate change so much because it makes us feel like we've become untethered, like we're drifting in the wind when we yearn to have our feet on the ground. In such times, you can abate your fear by remembering what the change *won't* change about you or the world around you that's important (like your connection with your family, your core values, your commitment to serve others, your desire to become the best possible version of yourself, or your *Star Wars* action-figure collection). By keeping ourselves grounded in this way, we keep ourselves anchored to what matters and what can serve as a source of reassuring constancy, even in the face of painful change. As such, this is one anchor that doesn't weigh you down, it lifts you up.

5. *Bring order to unruly change.* I've often experienced that people aren't afraid of change as much as they're afraid of not being prepared for change. You can make change considerably less intimidating by being proactive and having a plan for ushering yourself through change. Give the change structure, break it into manageable pieces, develop supporting routines to quickly reground yourself in the familiar, and revisit your plan regularly. Research shows that repetition in reviewing how and why you're changing and what the associated consequences of success or failure are will increase the probability of successfully navigating that change.[44]

6. *Get clear on the case for change.* No one likes to make sacrifices and go through something painful without knowing why they're doing it (other than mosh-pit aficionados). Nine times out of ten, you're owed clarity on the *why* behind the change that lays before you. But don't wait around for it—go get it. Seek to understand the

link to the broader business goals and then to your personal goals, values, and identity. Understand the short- and long-term wins involved. To help strengthen the case for change, find healthy dissatisfaction with the way things are, thus setting up the ensuing change as necessary. Imagine what's at stake if you don't undergo the change.

7. *Get yourself involved in the change.* Make it your business to get involved in the business of change. Change agents who help transition in the new reality are always welcomed by the initiators of change, and are quite often among the most informed. Increasing your IQ on the change at hand will reduce the anxiety afoot. And championing change versus cowering from it can create a vastly sunnier outlook. I've heard it said and found it true that unhappy people fear change while happy people create positive change.

8. *Have real faith, not blind faith.* Related to the first two items on this list, but worthy of its own mention is the distinction between real faith and blind faith. Blind faith is when you believe things will just work out, but not of your own accord—like expecting last year's string of Christmas lights to actually work. You believe some other force will make it so, and that you don't need to do anything. Real faith is when you understand you have a unique role in things, take responsibility accordingly, and believe that your commitment and abilities will carry you through. You are stoic in your resolve and eager to help mold the outcome.[45]

9. *Focus on what you can control.* Yes, this is a platitude. But then why don't we do it? The truth is that while much of the change around you may be out of your control, you can control your attitude toward the change itself.

FEAR OF CRITICISM

The fear of criticism is the final of the three most debilitating, inspiration-draining, incarnations of fear that we'll attack. We do so by first asking an odd question.

What makes a critic tick?

By this I mean what is the underlying motivation of the professionals who review movies, books, or theater?

Is it to provide the basic service of guiding our choice on how to spend our free time and money? Sure—that's the easy answer most of us would offer.

But what would such critics themselves tell you about their motivations?

Award-winning theater critic Albert Williams once answered this question in a keynote to his fellow critics. He said that "critics believe the creators of the art really want feedback, of any kind. They see their role as a teacher, and teachers challenge the material they are discussing. They see themselves as reporters, boosters, and skeptics, all *to create better art.*" [46]

Do we view our own critics the same way?

Do we see them as trying to create better art, in the form of a better version of ourselves?

Odds are, no.

Instead, we are more likely to fear their observations. And once again, the way our brain is wired plays a part in our predisposition to not only feel, but dwell, on this fear.

Studies prove that we are four times more likely to remember negative criticism than praise (true even among happy people) and that bad feedback is processed more thoroughly than good.

Such is the extent to which negative events impact us that psychology professor Roy Baumeister says it takes our brain experiencing five positive events to make up for the psychological effect of just one negative event.[47] (Unless that one negative event was a Jonas Brothers concert—good luck recovering any time soon.)

So our wiring works against us in regards to criticism, and inspiration thus faces another natural enemy. But that's no cause for despair—here's help.

Ten Ways to Overcome the Fear of Criticism

1. *Know that anything worth doing attracts admiration* and *criticism.* Would you rather be judged or ignored? These are the consequences of life's great binary choice—whether to make a difference, or not. Faced with this decision, surely taking on some criticism seems acceptable in comparison. If you want to "dent the universe," as Steve Jobs once challenged, you're going to take dents in your armor here and there. No one said it was fair. In fact, one of life's great imbalances is the fact that what others risk by criticizing is miniscule compared to what you risk by putting yourself out there (Internet trolls I'm looking at you). But don't let that stop you. Don't *ever* let that stop you. Inspiration is drawn to the labor of your legacy.

2. *Be clairvoyant about avoidance.* When it comes to criticism, a strategy of avoidance is more damaging than you might realize. Aristotle once said, "There is only one way to avoid criticism: do nothing, say nothing, and be nothing."[48] You must realize that avoiding criticism is what makes you weaker, not the criticism itself, and that such avoidance means you are withholding your gifts from the world. You simply can't let your fear of criticism outweigh your desire for success. As web television host Marie Forleo put it, "Will you ever say on your deathbed: 'whew, I avoided criticism?'"[49]

3. *Seek improvement, not approval.* When you adopt this philosophy, you're drawn to criticism as a cradle of insight instead of steering away from it as a source of rejection. Consider what is constructive about criticism, find the nugget of truth in it, and let

it elevate you to higher standards. Don't think of it as exposing flaws but instead as helping you make new self-discoveries. Let criticism feed you, not your insecurities.

4. *Consider the intent of the criticism.* Criticism is either intended to help you or hurt you. Identifying if the former is true can be freeing. The latter ain't easy, but remember this—such criticism is often more about them, than you. They may be projecting their own fears or inadequacies. Unfortunately, some people have a nasty habit of tearing others down when they're not being built up themselves. Compartmentalize that kind of input for what it is. For the hybrid situation where it's meant to be helpful, but isn't, view that criticism as merely giving you information about the inclinations and perspective of the giver. And for the nastiest of it, live by this: "Ignore the boos. They usually come from the cheap seats."[50]

5. *If you can't control the sting, keep it from swelling.* Even with the best of mindsets, that initial moment when we're receiving criticism can still sting. How you react from that instance forward can mean the difference between that sting persisting and swelling, or quickly abating. The key is not to get overemotional or overreact. The vast majority of the time the criticism is not meant to be a personal attack—it's not about you; it's about your work or your behavior. Most important, you control the pain from criticism when you remember the following: You can't change the words that were spoken to you, but you can change the meaning you give to them. You can rise above any words.[51] (Except "Sorry, we're out of chocolate cake.")

6. *Decide who gets to criticize you.* Not all criticizers are created equal, and some shouldn't even get a seat at the table. Set criteria for those who make the cut, and mentally dismiss the rest (they'll thus be too busy pounding sand to criticize you anymore). Mentors are a particularly good choice for those on the short list,

because they can give you practice receiving criticism in a safe environment, making it a less frightful experience over time.

7. *Let our elders inspire you.* You need to look no further for a role model in facing criticism then the older generation all around you. Ever notice how your grandmother doesn't care who says what about her? (Or that your secrets are safe with her because she can't remember them?) Those who've been on the planet longer tend to feel they have nothing to prove, no longer seek validation, and are more likely to have cemented a sense of self-belief and self-worth. Experience has shown them what they're capable of withstanding, and with fewer years ahead of them, reception of criticism is both fleeting and filed accordingly. This is one area of your life where getting ahead of yourself is not a bad thing.

8. *Get your skeletons out of the closet.* No I don't mean come clean about taking office supplies home every night as part of your retirement plan. What I mean is this: We fear criticism when we fear it will expose flaws that we want no one to know about. If you have a good enough relationship with your boss, share the things you know you aren't good at and want to improve upon—especially the things that are toughest to admit. Or find a coworker to do this with. The point is to get out in the open with someone the things you most fear getting criticized for. Doing so will not only get you working on those things but will also lessen the blow when those very flaws are being illuminated by someone else.

9. *Recall when criticism helped an outcome.* We lessen our fear of criticism when we recall instances when criticism led to a better way forward. Think of the last few times you were criticized, or criticized someone else with good intent. Odds are, *something* improved because of those critical remarks.

10. *Stay focused on the conclusion, not the criticism.* When you keep what you're trying to accomplish in front of you at all times, you'll speed through the sidebar of criticism. Renowned race car driver Mario Andretti once shared his number one secret to his success in the sport: "Don't look at the wall. Your car goes where your eyes go." This reminder is particularly poignant when it comes to our fear of criticism. If we take our eyes off the road ahead and what we're trying to achieve, and instead focus it on the walls of potential criticism all around us, we'll steer right into those walls.[52] Our misplaced focus on the criticism may well cause us to alter our actions and crash into an outcome that attracts the very criticism we feared in the first place. So steer clear of such self-fulfilling focus.

The Anti-Muse of Fear can, and must, be banished. You now have the insight to counter this antithesis of inspiration.

To Fear I say this: Your mindset warping power is officially eviscerated and your grip on us is hereby relinquished.

Inspiration and encouragement, get your rain boots on—we're about to run a marathon.

3

Settling and Boredom
(REJECTED)

I OFTEN WONDER why we're called human beings.

We should be called humans doing. Go, go, go, do, do, do—we are so caught up in our routines, our responsibilities, our commitments that we barely have any time to be, let alone become. It's all too easy to get stuck in a rut at work (and in life), a state where all we become is complacent, where we don't hold high hopes for things changing for the better or for our ability to affect that change, and where our meaningful output plummets.

Evidence is particularly ample on this last piece. A Gallup poll shows an astonishing 70 percent at work are disengaged. Relatedly, studies by Microsoft and AOL show that *up to 40 percent* of time spent at work is wasted, unproductive time—a by-product of a lulled and bored workplace.[1] And that's one of the more conservative estimates I unearthed.

That's a whole lot of records stuck in a groove on the turntable of life.

It's time to change the tune.

The Anti-Muse of Settling and Boredom has been lazily humming her siren song in your ear for too long now.

You have the power to get yourself unstuck—and to rekindle a burning desire for new stimuli in your life.

You just need a little know-how and an attitude of no-more.

Your resolve will pay dividends in your pursuit of vim and vigor. Leading researchers on inspiration have pinpointed "openness to experiences" as the single factor that most correlates with facilitating feelings of inspiration.[2]

It starts with your commitment to the Settling and Boredom Salvo in Figure 3-1. I'd issue it to you as a court order if I could. But it would probably just show up at your place right after you put your sweatpants on for the evening, so you wouldn't answer the door anyway.

FIGURE 3-1
THE SETTLING AND BOREDOM SALVO

- *I will take responsibility*—Unstuck starts with *U*. You have to realize you're in a rut before you can pull yourself out of one. American humorist Will Rogers said "The road to success is dotted with many tempting parking spaces." Be honest with yourself if you've put it in "park" and take ownership to get it back in "drive."

- *I will ascertain the pattern, then airlift myself out*—When we get stuck, by definition we're caught in a pattern of some sort. This is about being self-aware enough to recognize the specifics of the pattern that you've fallen into and the corresponding habits that are weighing you down. If someone else was examining your behaviors that have you stuck, what would they point out? Are you repeatedly telling yourself "just a few more years of this"? Are you continually avoiding new challenges when they arise or dodging conversations with friends on how you're doing? The critical first step is to embrace a state of awareness about the patterns and behaviors that have you stuck. Then, and only then, can you change your behaviors and begin working to yank yourself out of it.

- *I will recommit to the concept of challenge*—Think of what it means to challenge—it's to put opposition against or test the abilities of something. When we're stuck in a rut, we tend to push the very idea of challenge out of our peripheral zone so we can numbly stay in our false comfort zone. We're in a mode of repetition and path of least resistance. We aren't challenging much of anything—our assumptions, the status quo, or ourselves. We weren't always like this—we can remind ourselves of how exhilarating it is to be challenged by simply starting with a small, doable challenge. But mostly, just start—think of challenge as a curious notion in and of itself and pique your interest in the idea and its potential once again.

- *I will get "next" going*—It's hard to change course if you don't have a destination. We can get stuck at times simply because we haven't envisioned the next reenergizing step in our path. But you have to take that first step on what's next to move things from a rut to a reinvigorating route. It's time to take risks, embrace learning and growth experiences, and create your own opportunities.

Before we get going on "getting next going," let me first be seemingly contradictory for a moment. I'd like to make an argument that there are times when we *should* settle at work.

Philosophy professor Robert Goodin points out that settling at times is "intrinsic to living any kind of meaningful existence because virtually all human activity requires some stability, some fixed points, some closed-off options". Accept a job and it's important to commit to it for a time instead of continually scanning the landscape for better options (unless you just took a job at Blockbuster Video or Circuit City). Thus, we actually can't function without some level of settling. The problem arises when we don't follow Goodin's advice to periodically *check in on the balance of settling versus striving in your professional career.*[3]

What follows are how to's for three of the most powerful ways to rebalance things back toward striving and away from settling (and the boredom that comes with it). I'll discuss how to embolden yourself to take more risks, how to get learning and growing again, and how to make your own opportunities. You soon won't have to settle for anything less than inspiration.

HOW TO EMBOLDEN YOURSELF TO TAKE MORE RISKS

As we take risks and try new things, we expand our horizons and get exposed to more. Our fear of the unknown diminishes as a result and we're more likely to try yet more new things.

As we broaden our horizons, we narrow our inhibitions.

What a wonderful virtuous cycle.

So, what holds us back?

For certain, many of us are working more in a culture of caution than courage. A study conducted by Blessing White found that 41 percent of employees said their manager never encouraged them to take risks, while another 33 percent said their manager only sometimes encouraged them to take risks.[4] Behind this reluctance may lie fear, born from precedent or perception, of the negative consequences of failure.

Perhaps we don't account for the cost of status quo, we don't feel equipped to succeed when we do take risks, or we don't feel we have the capacity to invest the effort it can take to see a risk through. Maybe the poison of practicality seeps into our veins— "I'd like to go for it, but realistically...."

Or maybe we don't live our lives as if on any given flight someone *won't* switch their phone to airplane mode.

Anyway, whatever the culprit, one thing's for certain.

When our hesitance rules the day, inspiration can't be our knight (see what I did there?).

You can start small in risk-taking. You can go big. Either way, the wonderful freedom from familiarity you'll experience will encourage more and more risk-taking.

Here's how to get going.

Twelve Tactics to Encourage Risk-Taking

1. *Get clear on the rules of risk-taking.* If you've ever been in a casino, you'll often notice crowds around one game station in particular—the craps table. Craps is played with dice on a large, oval sunken table that is covered with a series of colorful, albeit confusing-looking, markings. It's a social game; on some rolls of the dice everyone wins (inducing round robin high-fives— which, and let's be honest, is primarily done by us air-guitaring, Neanderthal-simplistic men), and certainly the cheers draw a host of onlookers. But gaming industry experts will also tell you that craps has one of the lowest throughput rates, meaning watchers tend to pile up and watch (clogging the casino floor) versus jumping in and actually playing. In truth, the game is quite intimidating to watch and learn. The onlookers don't understand the rules, and so are hesitant to jump in and roll the dice, literally.

The same is true of risk-taking in the workplace. Risk-taking seems scary because we don't understand the "rules of the game." What constitutes a smart risk or a dumb one? Who needs to approve a risk to be taken? What happens in the face of failure or success? How does one get support along the way to increase odds of success?

Defining the rules of engagement in risk-taking up front and giving it some structure can greatly defuse inhibitions. If you're a manager of others, provide this framing. If you're an employee, ask for it.

You might be thinking, "Yeah but my boss/bosses are too conservative. Bottom line is they don't like to take risks."

First, let me say that you're hardly alone if you find yourself in this scenario.

Research broadly backs this assertion up. For example, one global organization that considered itself highly supportive of new product development polled its employees on what they thought would happen if the employees tried out new, unproven ideas. The answer surprised the brass, even if it doesn't surprise us worker bees. Only 17 percent of employees said that such behavior would be rewarded or approved while a whopping 47 percent said that the reaction from their superiors would be "unpredictable."[5] And frankly, we've all probably experienced environments where an "unpredictable" reaction would be a best-case scenario.

So, I get it. There's a good chance you work in a culture of caution versus courage.

But here's the thing.

If you were to say to anyone, even a conservative boss, "I'd like to talk to you about the rules of risk-taking," there's zero percent chance he/she will say in response "The rules are never, ever, take a risk. Period."

Who would say that?

No one.

The point is, framing your discussion around wanting to understand the rules of risk-taking will get the conversation going in a nonthreatening way and will help illuminate any possible degrees of freedom you might have.

2. *Start a small brushfire.* Here's another option if you're faced with a conservative chain of command that doesn't value or reward risk-taking, or worse, even punishes it.

The idea is to start changing the attitude toward risk-taking by starting small and slowly fanning the flames. Start with a request to do some experimentation, just to get risk-taking more familiar and in the DNA of the place. Be clear on the business case for the experiment and set clear rules, budgets, and timelines. Leverage the argument of organizational expert Salim Ismail who believes that some form of risk-taking is a must in today's organization and who said that "Mark Zuckerberg agrees, noting, 'The biggest risk is not taking any risk.' Constant experimentation and process iteration are now the only ways to reduce risk."[6] Celebrate and share the results if the risk pans out, and if it doesn't, be downright enthusiastic about what's been learned, talking about it to management as a process of paying tuition.

Indeed, Thomas Watson Jr. of IBM famously told an employee who feared he was about to be terminated after a 10 million dollar mistake, "Fire you? Why would I fire you? We've just spent 10 million dollars educating you!"[7] (Rumor has it Watson did, however, take away the employee's corporate frequent-flier miles.)

The idea is to demonstrate that when risk-taking is rewarded, the company will be rewarded right back. Such positive exposure to risks starts to soften the edges, open up minds, and slowly encourages more risk-taking.

3. *Create risk pools.* Related to the above, to help stimulate an environment more conducive to risk-taking, especially in the face of a risk-averse culture, form risk pools. That is, form a small cluster with some of your peers and get empowered to take risks. The common experience of navigating unchartered territory will yield bonding and a spirit of figuring things out together, and will improve the chances of a successful outcome. The process of taking risks thus becomes less scary through shared experience, and will ultimately produce more of the desired risk-taking behavior. Plus, you'll have more friends you can send "Don't break this chain!" emails to during the workday.

4. *Get the math right.* Believe it or not, math can get in the way of our risk-taking. Research indicates that we consistently overestimate the consequences of taking a risk, while we discount the

cost of status quo.[8] So be realistic in your assessment of what can go wrong and the penalty for so doing, including an honest assessment of whether or not what could be lost is in truth merely superficial. And don't blow off the cost of doing nothing. Leave that for slackers still living in their parents' basement.

5. *Identify your irrational behaviors.* An aversion to risk-taking is often fed by our irrational behaviors. You may have an excessive need for certainty or an unreasonable need to play it safe.[9] You may be overly concerned about looking foolish or have an overwhelming need for control. You may be an unrealistic pleaser, not wanting to let anyone down by your attempts at something new, all while being saddled by your own insane expectations. Only you know your insecurities (you and Amazon probably, since they know so much about you already).

The point is to consciously put these irrationalities (and we all have them) front and center and then exit them stage left.

6. *Be inspired by the end user.* When we reconnect with the people who benefit from the products or services we administer, it gives us newfound inspiration to take risks on their behalf.

I did a keynote once for a medical devices company that brings users of their products on stage at the annual meeting. Everyone in the company gets inspired by the personal stories of how the company's products made a difference to those individuals. Then, they follow up the feel-good the next day with a "Risk for Reward" session. Teams brainstorm what risks they can take to quicken the development of future products/improvements for the very end user they were inspired by the previous day.

Reconnecting with the end user can also uncover unmet or previously unarticulated needs that will require risk-taking to fulfill, thus providing further inspiration. And it gives you an excuse to travel to cool cities to do focus groups.

7. *Think of risk-taking as a skill that must be built.* No different from visioning or strategic thinking, risk-taking is an essential skill required for success, self-confidence, and even for setting you apart from others. Go so far as to set risk-taking as an expectation of yourself.

Sara Blakely, the billionaire founder of Spanx, a women's shapewear company, says she learned to appreciate the value of smart risk-taking because her dad asked her and her brother the same question every Friday at dinner—"What have you failed at this week?"[10] (I, on the other hand, was asked "What haven't you failed at this week?")

8. *Set a high bar.* Big expectations for results will naturally encourage risk-taking. Similarly, expecting much from one's mindset—setting the self-expectation to act like a thought leader for your industry, for example, will inspire bold attempts and set new standards.

9. *Plan to succeed.* We can become averse to risks because of bad experiences in the past with risks gone wrong. Peeling back the onion further, research indicates that often risks go wrong because we were too timid in how we carried out that risk, letting caution and worry ride shotgun. So, attack the risk like you mean to succeed. Have an explicit plan. Get the resources, background knowledge, and preparation all in place and when in, go all-in. Don't let your doubts and worries become self-perpetuating; your mother-in-law will take care of that for you.

10. *Resist your neurological "no."* I talked earlier about starting a small brushfire to counter ingrained resistance. This point is about resisting your *own* neurological no and not shutting down risk-taking of your own accord too quickly. This is easier said than done, as we have an almost electrical impulse embedded in us to say no in the face of risks.

Robert Goldberg, former managing director of Idealab, noted that in large organizations if multiple managers are initially supportive of a risky idea but just one manager resists, most often the resistance will cause a ripple effect just strong enough to kill the idea.

So, the odds are already stacked in favor of a risk being dead on arrival. Don't worsen it.

To protect its organization from such stifling risk aversion, Amazon has put in place the "institutional yes"—any manager wanting to say no to a subordinate's great idea must write a two-page document explaining why he or she is against the idea. Thus, the company has put friction behind saying no, leading to the test and implementation of more new ideas.[11]

11. *Role model a safe haven for hearing ideas.* The inspiration to take risks often comes from the birth of exciting new ideas. Create an incubator for such inspired risk by helping to promote an environment of open, risk-free idea sharing. Exposure to more great ideas will encourage you and your teammates to take more risks to advance those ideas. Cast a wide net for participants in the idea-sharing and have low tolerance for idea-bashing. This is one area where you really do hold the power—you can role model your way to a culture change. Even the most oppressive, conservative manager will have a hard time finding a reason to shut down a grassroots effort among the troops to practice open idea-sharing.

12. *Double down at risk-taking breaking points.* The process of risk-taking will run into natural stress points that can derail the entire process. For example, zeal for taking smart risks can wane in the face of layers of approval required, when things aren't going as planned or preliminary failure is evident, or when tradition is raising its head and making it difficult to cast old risk-averse behaviors aside.

Know going into the risk to be taken that these tension points might arise. Be on the lookout for such tensions and be prepared to ask for air cover or for a doubling down on commitment and support to keep things moving forward.

HOW TO GET LEARNING AND GROWING AGAIN

Your brain is desperate to get out more.

I mean like Cinderella in a cult compound desperate to get out more.

I know this because it rewards us tremendously when we rub its belly and open it up to new experiences every now and then.

A study done by the Kellogg School of Management showed that those who travel abroad have shown higher levels of creativity, greater open-mindedness to different ideas, and better identification of multiple solutions to problems.[12]

All because the study participants let their brains roam in Rome.

A study by the University of Michigan showed that taking a stroll in nature can boost your cognitive performance (memory and attention) *by more than 20 percent*.[13]

Warren Buffett, on his best day, couldn't have gotten you that kind of return on investment.

So, c'mon—can we throw our brain a bone please? Frankly, it's just unbecoming to see it begging at the table. Feeding it new stimuli in a way that quells its hunger, opens up inspiration, and jump-starts learning and growth again involves two components—*intent that ignites* and *approaches that accelerate*.

Intent That Ignites

No one overtly chooses to stop learning and growing again; it just kind of happens in the deluge of daily responsibilities (and life). And if it were easy to kick it into gear again, you would have already done it.

I can help.

I offer research-backed insight on how clarity of intent—a specific set of intentions in fact—can serve as ignition to get you over the hump. Here are some powerful prompts to get you gung ho on learning and growth again, thus opening up inspiration as a joyous by-product.

- *Seek conscious growth (becoming who you are) versus growth for the sake of it*[14]—The latter is a hobby; the former is a homecoming. Odds are if you really love learning and growing, as if it were a hobby, you probably don't need my insight to recommit to it. Lack of time or other common factors are simply getting in the way, or you'd be doing more of it, because you love it. If merely reading this reminds you of how much you love it and you recommit to it accordingly—fantastic. But I'm offering something more compelling. View the process of pursuing growth as a critical step in the journey of becoming who you really are, what you were meant to be. We'd all like more time for our hobbies. But we all simply *must make time* for becoming the best possible version of ourselves. Not to do so is a travesty, not a mere sidetrack. Raise the stakes.

- *Dread obsolescence*—I shared in my last book, *Make It Matter,* that pioneers of learning organizations believe that the rate of change in many industries is now so great that the only competitive advantage left may be the very rate at which its constituents are able to learn, grow, and change. So, future proof yourself and slap back stagnation like the drunken frat boy that it is. Recognize that the need to up your skills is central to maintaining your livelihood, and to feeling like you are contributing your best effort. We are more likely to self-inspire when we are more self-assured.

- *Let your values vault you forward*—The values we hold sacred can deeply motivate us. Frame your learning and growing as an opportunity to better serve your values.

  For example, perhaps a core value of yours is servitude

to others. What can you learn to better serve? Or perhaps you hold dear the value of kindness. What might you learn or who could you study that would help you more consistently show up as kind and caring (other than Hello Kitty)?

Value-incentivized learning is some of the most powerfully motivated and inspiration-inducing learning we can muster. Give it a try.

- *Work* on *your life versus* in *your life*—What if I told you that recommitting to learning and growth could feed a sense of greater control in your life?

When you do so, it gives you a sense you're working on a better life for yourself and are escaping the hamster wheel of daily life we can all so easily get caught up in.

Some of the best employees I've ever had (a) picked up my dry cleaning, and (b) worked *on* the systems they labored in (to make them better), versus just *in* them—it's no different for us with our own lives. We can work *on* our best lives by learning and growing throughout, and basking in the significance of so doing, rather than just looking back one day and realizing we've merely been living *in* our life as it was happening to us.

To assist in this, it's critical to be disciplined enough to spend less time on the maintenance tasks in your life, and more time on the growth tasks in your life.

Research by Anders Ericsson, a leading cognitive science and performance excellence expert, supports this. Ericsson's studies on growth and expertise, whose subject matters ranged from typists to elite athletes, indicated that rote repetition of a skill, no matter how much, clearly plateaued one's growth. It was the *deliberate practice*, working on specific tasks that would grow and stretch, like technique, that led to true growth.[15]

And so it is with all of us when we spend more time on tasks that we know will stretch us.

Which brings us to this next part.

Approaches That Accelerate

OK, so you've clarified and powerfully reframed your reason for learning and growing. Now let's throw gas on the fire. Here are some time-tested approaches that can get growing going.

- *Discern between good and great, then get after the latter*—Oftentimes we stunt our growth because we simply don't truly understand the difference between what good and great looks like. Thus, we spend our time on a murky "good enough" that doesn't really grow and stretch us.

  Think about it. Can you truly say that right now, for every project you're invested in or for every critical performance vector related to your job, that you really understand how your boss would define what great looks like?

  Many of us guess or simply don't ask.

  Take the time to sit down with your boss and get really clear on what good is, and what great is, then embrace and work toward the latter. Doing so will stretch you and invite learning, growing, and inspiration in.

  The table that follows is an extremely effective tool I've used many times to powerful effect. The left-hand column contains a list of performance attributes that are typically quite important for success in business (you can also list key project outcomes desired here). Then, I very specifically define with my people or with my boss (it works both ways) what good looks like and what great looks like. I mean I literally write it out, like in the table. It doesn't matter if you agree or not with my sample definitions in this table; it's much more important that you use the table to conduct the exercise yourself. You'll be amazed at how it can change what you spend your time on, and how inspired you are by that expenditure.

THE GOODNESS/GREATNESS GRID

KEY PERFORMANCE VECTOR	GOODNESS	GREATNESS
Leadership	You work hard at leadership. You get things done. Your cross-functional partners and direct reports like working with you.	You can't help but lead because others want to follow.
Thinking & Acting Decisively	You make firm decisions, with sufficient data in hand.	You make firm decisions, with sufficient data *and* stakeholders in hand (*people need to weigh in before they can buy in*).
Getting Things Done	You make things happen.	You make the right things happen, before you're asked. And you over-invest in leaving footprints (*legacy work*).
Risk-Taking	You let fear smartly temper your risk-taking—well thought through, calculated risks only, please.	You fear not taking calculated risks.
Priority Setting	*- Trash compactor management -* You brutally prioritize and compact your workload, focusing on delivering the most important things.	*- Accordion management -* You continually re-prioritize, contracting and expanding your workload by adding more high-value work, taking off low-value work, and flowing to surges.
Capacity	You personally take on and crank through any priority you're given.	You make it personal for others to take on as well.
Strategic Thinking	You consistently lead management's thinking.	You consistently lead, and largely finish, management's thinking (*with thorough, strategic thought*).
Intelligence	You have great intelligence (IQ).	You have great emotional intelligence (EQ) as well.
Attention to Detail	You have an eye for detail.	You helicopter up and down fluidly.

continued . . .

KEY PERFORMANCE VECTOR	GOODNESS	GREATNESS
Problem Solving	You consistently solve problems with solid thinking.	You bring problems management didn't know they had, along with solutions (*beating snakes out of the grass*).
Vision I	You set clear, inspiring visions.	You set the vision with the end state clearly in mind— and set a course to connect the dots in between. You over communicate your vision.
Vision II	You thoroughly understand the vision for your products/category/ division and make smart supporting decisions.	You routinely think beyond your title.
Follow Through	You follow through on the important things with excellence, and pick and choose the rest.	You follow through relentlessly—even if it's to say you aren't following through. You inspire an unwavering sense of confidence that you've "got it covered."
Organizational Contributions	You've made significant contributions working *in* the system and improving "the smell of the place."	You've also led unexpected contributions working *on* the system that have changed the DNA of the place.
Growing Capability in Others	You invest in your people—they'd all say they've learned from you.	You've become a "destination category."

- *Introduce new stimuli*—If a stroll in the park or a little travel can produce the cognitive benefits described earlier, imagine what introducing a portfolio of new stimuli could do. Try a podcast. Have lunch with someone whose job is nothing like yours. Find a blog you like and follow it (I won't be mad if it's mine you choose at scottmautz.com). Sign up for an online course. Heck, try shoplifting (not really though). The idea here is to expose yourself to a number of new things to learn from and see what it sparks. You can choose to learn a little about a lot of things, or focus on a few things and penetrate them to build up a deeper mastery. Either approach might even invite some wide-eyed wonder back into your life.

- *Unplug others' opinions*—Learn what you want to learn. Grow where you want to grow. Everyone else can stuff it—why should they slow you down? And with this approach you won't be afraid to start from where you are right now in your learning journey on whatever topic you take on. Pretenses are for pretenders (and free-trade specialty coffee drinkers). You're just trying to become a better, more inspired version of your genuine self.

- *Link with learners*—Some people just love to learn, which can be contagious (as opposed to those who just won't learn, which can be confounding). Anyway, seek the former out and find out what learning journey they're on and what feeds it. Get caught up in the practice with them. Or seek out the opportunity to work for a boss who will help you grow. You'll know who they are or can easily find out—it's such a coveted and valued skill set that people so blessed have nowhere to hide.

HOW TO MAKE YOUR OWN OPPORTUNITIES

With a title like "How to Make Your Own Opportunities" you're probably wondering if I'm going to swerve into self-help drivel: "You can do it!" "Just put your mind to it!" "Learn to sell real estate in just two hours!"

Look, I know how easy it would be to stigmatize a section on this, but the truth is, I think I can help. I've known many good souls with stunted trajectories who couldn't get past their belief that opportunities happen for people who are in the right place, right time. Period.

I'm sorry but that's just not so.

The truth is, good fortune comes to those who are fortunately good enough at *attracting* opportunity. If you suspect that's not you, don't despair. Here's a simple but effective tool I've used over the years called *The Window of Opportunity* (Figure 3-2). Let's throw it open and let the cool breeze of inspiration waft its way in.

FIGURE 3-2
THE WINDOW OF OPPORTUNITY

Carve out a niche and become a guru	Mine the downers for some uppers	Have a one-up attitude and a two-up ask
Breathe in the O_2	Mind your inner bat signal	Add value always

These six ways of making your own opportunities have proven to work for me and many with whom I've shared them, time and again. Let's look at each one.

1. *Carve out a niche and become a guru*—I was blessed enough to run several of Procter & Gamble's largest multi-billion-dollar businesses. No doubt, success in each of these opportunities led to more opportunities. But opportunities really came rolling in (of the sort I treasured most of all) when I carved out a niche for being the go-to guy in the company for inspirational leadership talks. I started with a single talk to a small group, and within a few years I was doing twenty-five to thirty talks a year to larger and larger audiences within

the walls of P&G as word-of-mouth spread. It allowed me to serve my fellow employees and continually hone my areas of expertise. It also gave me practice for when I'd eventually leave to pursue my great passion for speaking (and writing of course, dear reader). I invested to become an absolute expert at the leadership topics I covered and to deliver the material with zeal. The effort served as a launch pad for my second career, and the opportunities have been abundant ever since.

2. *Mine the downers for some uppers*—As it turns out, problems, frustrations, and adversity are a gold mine of opportunity.

   And if you're willing to be a miner, the opportunities are major.

   When we beat the snakes out of the grass (go looking for problems no one knew they had), they become opportunities insofar as you can develop highly valued solutions for them.

   Our frustrations become fodder for opportunity as well—they are essentially unrealized potential. Richard Branson started his own airline because he was so pissed off at his own travel experience.[16] Eric Betzing got so frustrated with the limitations of the microscope that he invented his own, and took home a Nobel Prize for the effort (as well as the floral arrangement from the banquet table that night).

   Adversity yields opportunity in two ways. First, it gives us the chance to reveal our true character and constitution when it counts most and will be most vividly remembered. Second, it is its own brand of problem to be solved with the exhibition of very special leadership required.

3. *Have a one-up attitude and a two-up ask*—Two parts to this one. First, when I say have a one-up attitude, I don't mean in a better than thou way. I mean it in a better

than before way. View everything you encounter in your job with curiosity; how could you make it one-click better, or even step-change, better? My electric teakettle worked just fine for me. But some inquisitive soul wondered if there was a more convenient way to get me my morning coping mechanism in a better fashion, and voilà—the Keurig machine, and a massive new category to boot.

A constant effort of looking for ways to one-up how well things are done today can lead to tremendous opportunity (but please note that adopting this attitude with your spouse leads to the opportunity to hire a divorce lawyer).

Now, while looking to one-up current practices, you can two-up what you ask for. By this I mean periodically ask for stretch opportunities, assignments, resources, and support that are so aggressive they require your boss's boss—your two-up—to approve. Stretch assignments can include roles where you have to build whole new skill sets, manage much more complexity and diversity, influence through personal power versus position power, or manage through tremendous adversity and change.

The bottom line is that having a mindset of asking for the moon from time to time can lead to a galaxy of opportunity.

4. *Breathe in the O2*—Here I mean breathe in the oxygen of two critical *O*'s: Open-mindedness and Optimism— common antecedents to that big third *O*, Opportunity.

Psychology professor Richard Wiseman indicates just how powerful open-mindedness can be in attracting opportunity. In one of Wiseman's studies, subjects were given a newspaper and asked to count the number of photographs within. Most subjects completed the task within minutes and dutifully reported that there were forty-three photos, which there were.

However, they were all so locked in on the task in front of them that none of the respondents noticed two important prompts: large type on the second page that read "Stop counting—there are 43 photographs in this newspaper," or even better, "Stop counting, tell the experimenter you've seen this and win $250." The fact that no one noticed either prompt meant that (a) Wiseman had more poker money after the study, and (b) the notion was supported that loosening up a bit, being more open-minded, flexible, and not so tunnel-vision locked in on your tasks can open up a broader, opportunity-laden field of vision.[17]

Wiseman also weighs in on the power of optimism with his research. He conducted an experiment in which he placed the same two chance opportunities in front of two different individuals—money placed on a sidewalk and the potential for an encounter with a well-connected businessman planted in a coffee shop. The first respondent, a fellow with an optimistic outlook, spotted and picked up the money and struck up a conversation with the businessman, leading to more positive outcomes. The second respondent, self-described as "unlucky," stepped right over the money without seeing it and kept to herself in the coffee shop.[18]

Holy self-fulfilling prophecy.

When optimism morphs into old-fashioned positivity, similar outcomes ensue. Researchers from the University of Toronto found that people in good moods take in more visual information than those in bad moods.[19]

So, breathe in the O2 and exhale opportunity and inspiration.

5. *Mind your inner bat signal*—The denizens of Gotham and the dapper Bruce Wayne all take notice when that bat signal appears in the sky, like a blazing beacon not to be ignored.

   Think of your intuition the same way—it's like your signal flare for significance.

   Keep your eyes open for opportunities, and when that flare of intuition goes up and your spidey-sense is tingling (wow—two superhero references in three sentences), get after it. Resist the temptation to ignore your intuition for the plethora of reasons that we do—be it practicality, overthinking it, getting talked out of it, whatever the reason. Follow that thread.

6. *Add value always*—This one is the most straightforward method for opening the Window of Opportunity, but it's too important to ignore. Adopt the mindset of always adding value in your interactions with others. Challenge yourself to hold to this standard. People want to share opportunities with people like this, plain and simple. And the more you expand your network of people you meet and serve, the more opportunities that will come your way.

So, what say the only thing we let settle is the dust after a good ol' whomping of that Settling and Boredom Anti-Muse.

Deal?

Good. Because I think the bat signal just went up from an inundated individual in the next chapter. To the Batmobile!

4

Inundation

(RELIEVED)

SOMEWHERE ALONG THE way, overwhelmingly busy became the new black.

The research nerd in me wants to lay it on thick here, peppering you with study after study that proves all the negative effects this social bragging right is having on our health and well-being. The Anti-Muse of Inundation would probably appreciate the press. But let's not give her the satisfaction.

You know the deal. We're inundated and exhausted. This reality stifles progress, our sense of mastery, and our feelings of preparedness. Check.

What you may not be aware of, though, is how detrimental all of this is specifically to our ability to attract inspiration.

So let me get my geek on just a bit and share the following. Psychology research shows that when we make progress, it inspires us to set more inspirational goals. The fact that those goals are inspirational greatly spurs further progress on those goals (versus goals that aren't as inspiring).[1] Thus, when we're inhibited from making progress at work, it interrupts this critical cycle of self-inspiration.

Research also shows that when we're demonstrating mastery over our work and feeling prepared (instead of feeling overwhelmed) inspiration is much more likely to flourish. Indeed, as leading researchers have pointed out, "inspiration favors the prepared mind."[2]

We can become overwhelmed for many reasons—I mean like shopping the toothpaste aisle overwhelmed.

Likewise, many things can cause us to feel a lack of progress, mastery, or preparedness. The most common contributors to all these aspects of inundation are that we aren't good at making choices or setting priorities, we let procrastination or perfectionism get the better of us, or we don't know how to push back and/ or ask for help.

You can fight back against all of this and foster a more progress conducive, on-top-of-it environment. What follows are the how-to's.

HOW TO MAKE CHOICES AND SET PRIORITIES

In the world of marketing, any marketer worth his or her salt knows that a brand can't stand for everything. You have to carefully choose what the brand will do, say, and be. Otherwise focus is lost, the promise that the brand offers becomes muddled, and people will stop buying, and buying into, the brand.

The same goes for you. You too can lose focus, lose support, and lose your mind if you aren't disciplined about choosing what work you'll take on for yourself and/or others. Not making choices means people won't know what you stand for or what's important to you. Like a brand, it's much more difficult to make a real impact when you're spread too thin and trying to do too much. And everyone involved becomes exhausted, like 7 p.m. Friday night exhausted (anyone under 35, I don't expect you to get that joke).

Don't choose the easy thing by doing everything.

Too many managers are choosing this path. Research indicates that nearly one out of every two employees feels that the amount of work they're being asked to do is unreasonable.[3]

So inspiration isn't the only thing being buried.

As for you, whether you're a manager of others or not, you have to be conscious of your own bandwidth. And that means being hard on your work, which is hard work. But making disciplined choices is work you simply must take on.

Here's how.

Seven Methods to Help Make Choices and Prioritize

1. *Make a pact for impact.* Promise yourself you'll only work on what matters most, what will make the biggest impact on your core objectives. Articulate your winning aspiration and how the work you take on will feed it—if it's not helping you win, then it's making you lose (I totally just channeled my inner Vince Lombardi there). Keep your "or not's" in front of you. Will the new work contribute to your winning aspiration, or not? Will it contribute to your objectives, goals, and strategies, or not? If the answer is no, you know what to do.

Work on having 20/20 vision—meaning, work on the first 20 percent that adds the most value, and keep sight of the next 20 percent you can't get to but that you'd like to migrate above the cut line should the opportunity arise.

Another filter you can use is to ask yourself if the work is not just warranted, but worthy. Lots of work is warranted, but that doesn't mean you should do it all. Is it truly worthy of your time, effort, and energy? Will it help enable a worthy goal?

By the way, all of this doesn't mean you shouldn't commit to maintenance work along the way—things that are the cost of entry to enabling you to keep working on the things that do matter. It's more broadly about keeping the pact with yourself to keep your portfolio of work dominated by high-impact tasks/projects.

2. *Think weights and measures.* Be honest about the weight of the work you're about to take on—stop and ask yourself how much work will it really take? It may be more than you think (like the admission price to a Disney theme park). How many resources will really be required? Measure the amount of time you think it will take, then double it, given the rule that things always take longer than you expect—a rule known as Hofstadter's Law.[4] (Hofstadter probably declared it after hiring a contractor to re-finish his basement.)

Anyway, if the new work still makes the cut, so be it. Such intentionality at least forces careful consideration versus flippant commitment.

3. *Ask "What's the cost of knowing?"* We often ask or are asked to do work just to cover the bases, just because it's something good to know. It gives a sense of security, perhaps it is even triggered by an unfortunate sense of insecurity. At such times, asking for everything isn't exhaustive thinking, it's exhaustively lazy thinking.

Whatever the cause, such careless requests can take many forms. It might be an ask for an analysis not rooted in a mission-critical task. Or it might be a request for some research just to verify what's already been learned (you probably don't need another focus group to confirm that "Senseless" is a horrible name for your new line of fragrance-free deodorants, for example).

We need to stop in such moments and ask, "What's the cost of knowing this?" Some other priority item won't get worked on. Precious time, energy, and even money might be getting diverted from much more important endeavors. In other words, it just might turn out that the cost is too high.

4. *Run your manager through the mill.* This just in: Your boss is often the source of new work creation. Assuming you have a good working relationship with him or her, respectfully ask a lot of clarifying questions about the new work. This can be hard to

do; most of us are pleasers—but you must do it. Make sure the juice is worth the squeeze or you at least get the rationale behind the request so you can keep other doers motivated. Be clear on what the priorities are, and use those priorities to push back on work that is peripheral in nature. Help your boss to understand that you're not shirking work, you're shoring up work—the most important work that will make the biggest difference. Even if nothing ends up getting taken off your plate, at least you'll feel heard—speaking truths about your workload out loud can be therapeutic. And your boss will have more awareness (and hopefully appreciation) of exactly what you're working on.

Or they'll remain as clueless as me at a fabric store, but at least you'll have tried.

You should also prioritize who gets to prioritize. Our workload balloons when lots of people get a vote on what we work on. Develop a work plan for you and/or your people and align it with the one person who gets a say in what you work on. Then flow new work requests through this funnel.

5. *Have a To Do list and a To Don't list.* When it comes to prioritizing and getting things done, it's hard to beat the power of a good ol' To Do list. Add one more thing to your notepad though, right behind it: a To Don't list. Write down the kinds of things that you want to avoid or that you tend to get sucked into (like buying raffle tickets from coworkers' children). This list then serves as a reminder to, well, don't. Research is clear on the power of writing down your goals (versus just keeping them in your head).[5] This power also applies to writing down goals of what not to do.

6. *Know that addition by subtraction really works.* We all intuitively know what research confirms: When we choose to do less, we accomplish much more. Wishful thinking tricks us into believing that if we take on and do more, more will get done.

Don't take the bait from your jokester brain. But do take heed of General Dwight D. Eisenhower's brain (that relayed to his mouth) what's come to be known as the Eisenhower Principle: The thing you should be taking on more of is the truly important; take on less of the distractingly urgent.

7. *When prioritizing, think accordion, not trash compactor.* Those expert at prioritizing tend to ebb and flow with the workload, expanding and contracting the workload depending on the conditions. The workload might expand during times of a big sales call, a key upper management review, or during a visit from one's in-laws, for example.

Anyway, then the workload contracts in times thereafter to help restore energy—expanding and contracting, like an accordion.

Contrast this to the trash compactor mentality, which seeks to continually reduce and "squish" the workload into a smaller and smaller mass. On the surface this would seem to be the definition of prioritization. The problem with this approach, however, is that it's rigid; you can miss real opportunities to make progress toward your objectives simply because you are actually being *too* brutal in prioritizing.

A more fluid mindset is better, as it gives you permission to take on important new work but still forces accountability to counterbalance the total portfolio of work at some point with some disciplined "no's" and workload reductions.

HOW TO STOP PROCRASTINATING
AND GET S#@! DONE

Procrastination is the silent henchman for Inundation. Studies show that we lose fifty-five productive days a year due to procrastination, *218 minutes a day* on average.[6] That sneaky bastard.

And stopping procrastination is harder than trying to pull the drawstring in our sweatpants back out when it gets sucked into the waistband.

The good news is that I'm able to share with you a research and experience-based method I've developed that has worked for me and many others I've shared it with. Let's take a stroll together down this productive path (Figure 4-1).

FIGURE 4-1
THE PATH THROUGH PROCRASTINATION

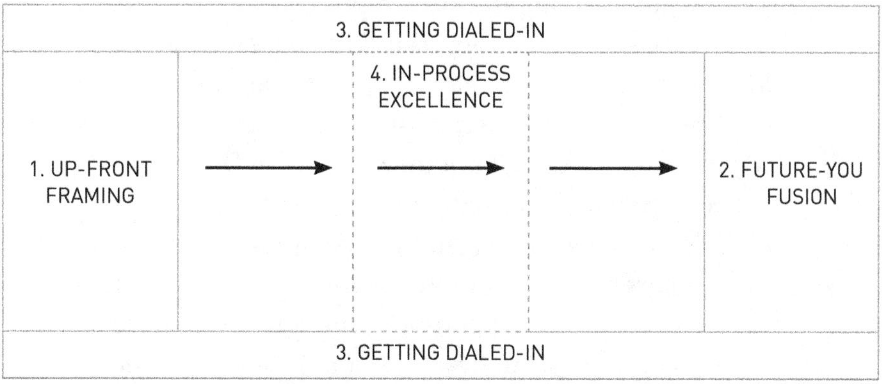

There are four phases on this path, depicted below: Let's break it down. Hammer style.

1. *Up-Front Framing*. The first phase involves some preliminary myth-busting and mindset-molding:

- Don't get sucked into these three misconceptions:
  a. *"I work better under pressure."* Research simply doesn't support this assertion. In fact, research shows just the opposite. Stress actually makes things much tougher on your brain, unduly loading it up and interfering with the ability to learn and translate ideas into meaningful information. In study after study, people under stress have repeatedly been shown to do more error prone work.[7] Yup. That's how I explain my SAT scores. Stress.

b. "My willpower will kick in." I know you want to believe that you'll get started on that task this weekend, or that you'll be able to resist watching your favorite show tonight so you can finish your presentation. Silly rabbit.

Unfortunately, studies show that our willpower isn't as strong as we tend to think it is and that it can be depleted surprisingly quickly. In fact, we often subconsciously avoid committing to long-term goals because we know deep down when we first encounter a setback, our willpower will quickly run out and we'll end up bailing. Think of that exercise routine you promised yourself you'd stick to. Things were going well until you missed two days in a row, then bam! Back to the usual.[8] Instead of exercising you exercise your right not to. Been there. Done that.

Even when we feel truly committed, we consistently believe that we have more restraint than we actually possess. Researchers from Northwestern's Kellogg School of Management conducted experiments on a range of temptations including greed, drug use, and arousal and found across the board that personal restraint levels were continually overestimated, leading to poor choices. This natural tendency spells trouble for the procrastinator.[9]

Don't despair, however—this is simply a cross-section of human nature. Help in stacking the deck back in your favor lies just ahead.

c. "My self-imposed deadlines will keep me on track." One last bit of tough love. Studies show that the idea of setting deadlines for yourself isn't as effective as you think it is.

Researchers Alberto Bisin and Kyle Hyndman gave word jumbles to different groups of students, with a promise of a cash payment if they completed the jumble on time (and nothing if they didn't). Groups were given one final deadline, a series of interim deadlines, or allowed to impose their own deadline. The group that imposed their own deadline was heavy with self-reported procrastinators who said they were using the opportunity for a self-imposed deadline to practice addressing their procrastination. It didn't matter, though—this group ultimately ended up having the lowest completion rate of any group. In reality, despite the self-imposed deadlines, they started the word jumbles too late, found out it was harder than they thought and that they didn't have enough time to complete, and so bailed on the task.

And so it often goes with such well-meaning procrastinators (and teenagers).

By the way, the group that did the best on task completion rate was the one working with a series of interim deadlines. This is consistent with other research that indicates setting such deadlines externally, like with a boss or with friends, is the most effective way to encourage adherence to a deadline.[10]

- Lay a groundwork of either pain or pleasure—The next bit of up-front framing needed on this path is to remember that you have to *feel* something to get going past procrastination. Indifference is poison.

  Pursuit of pleasure or avoidance of pain is just the kind of push we need to get going in many endeavors; it's no different with overcoming procrastination. Start by asking yourself, "Why do I need to get this task/project done?" Think of the pain that will be caused in the near term if you don't. (If there is no pain, by the way, then you may have a candidate for prioritization/making choices.) Think of the benefits in the near term to getting it done. Let either the potential pain or pleasure drive you.

  It also helps to ask yourself, "Why am I procrastinating?" Perhaps it's fear, boredom, displeasure for the task, or any number of things. Be honest with yourself, and when you discern the answer, find a positive to attach to the negative. Bored? Find ways to make it more interesting. You don't like doing the task? How can you spice up the task and add a little fun to the dread? Indifferent to the task? Clarify your goals and find the meaning and purpose behind the task at hand.

The key here is to not just numbly set the work aside once again in autopilot mode but to instead create stimuli to help jolt yourself into action. Think of it as Red Bull for your reticence.

- Forgive yourself—Interestingly enough, research indicates that one of the most powerful ways to get past procrastination is to first forgive yourself for procrastinating to begin with. Doing so eases guilt, which is one of the major causes of procrastination in the first place, as you want to avoid the uncomfortable feeling of confronting your utter lack of progress.

2. *Future-You Fusion.* The next phase in the path through procrastination involves some longer-term perspective. To get past procrastination it helps to emotionally connect with an image of yourself in the future, living as an action-oriented, procrastination-free version of you. While picturing future-you is important for overcoming any undesirable behavior, it is especially important for procrastinators. Not only do they put off taking action, they also tend to block out the implication of those inactions on the future-self. "I'll worry about that later," goes the thinking.

Fascinating research by UCLA psychologist Hal Hershfield supports this point and indicates that in general we have a difficult time making an emotional connection to our future-selves. In fact, we tend to see our future-selves as a different person altogether. In an experiment, Hershfield took MRI scans of subjects as they were asked to (a) think about themselves in the here and now, (b) think about themselves in a future state, and (c) think about celebrities like Natalie Portman or Matt Damon. The study showed that we use different parts of our brain to think about our current-selves and future-selves. Astonishingly, Hershfield reported that "the subjects' brain activity when describing their self in a decade was similar to when they were describing Natalie Portman."[11]

In other words, we see our future-self as someone else (not related to our current-self), and accordingly don't consider the gravity of our current actions on this stranger—poison for the procrastinator.

Procrastination researcher Timothy Pychyl contends that those who are more in touch with their future-selves are more likely to get past procrastination and just get on with things, as they want to make progress toward their desired version of future-self.[12]

So stop thinking of future-you as some other poor schlep—it's You 2.0, and what you do today (or not) affects the you of tomorrow and how fast you'll get there.

3. *Getting Dialed-In.* This phase on the path is depicted in the outer reaches of the diagram because it's about controlling the peripheral and getting down to business. Here's how:

- *Ditch the distractions*—You know what distracts you (besides Shark Week, I mean). Be intentional about keeping these distractions—especially of the digital variety—at bay. You intuitively know just how distracting your digital devices are, but let me put a number to it for you. The percent of people worldwide who can be coded as chronic procrastinators is now 25 percent, *5 times the rate* it was in the 1970s, before digital devices were prevalent.[13] Hmmm. See any correlation?
- *Beware the busywork*—You know the drill. Big meeting tomorrow that you need to finish prepping for? Better rearrange the apps on my phone first!

  Research indicates that our brain will attempt to simulate big, hairy productive work (after first avoiding it) by focusing instead on smaller, mindless tasks, thus giving the illusion that real work is being done.[14] Such little doses of mundane accomplishment can lead to other, similar small doses, pulling us further away from the intended task. Ever notice how that phone app rearrangement somehow leads to tidying the kitchen, which leads to organizing your closet? The key is to catch yourself in the act of this robotic behavior, evaluate each task you are engaging in, and then redirect your effort to the actual work that will get you back on course. Having everything you need to complete the task in front of you can also help keep you from straying.

4. *In-Process Excellence.* All right, in this final phase let's get down to doing the actual work at hand. What follows are a number of ways to help you work your way right past procrastination.

- *Put the Zeigarnik Effect to work for you*—This is my fancy way of saying how powerful it is to just . . . get . . . started. I'm not trying to be Captain Obvious here—check out the science behind this. Two eye-opening studies reveal what can happen if we just get a task under way.

  In one study, respondents were tested for their memory of doing easy cognitive tasks, like a puzzle. At one point, the researcher, Bluma Zeigarnik, interrupted the respondents and asked them to recall in detail the tasks they were doing or had already done. She discovered that people were twice as likely to recall more detail about tasks during which they were interrupted versus tasks they had completed. This has come to be known as the "Zeigarnik Effect," which states that we remember uncompleted tasks better than we do completed tasks—because uncompleted tasks nag at us.

  In the second study, participants had to solve a difficult puzzle in an unlimited amount of time. Before any of the participants were finished, they were told the study was over. Ninety percent of the study participants *kept working on the puzzle anyway.*

Why?

No, not because it was a jigsaw puzzle of a swimsuit model.

Because it nagged at them to leave the puzzle unfinished.

These two studies teach us that if we can manage to start a task, we're much more likely to remember it, and be driven to finish it.[15]

Our brain just works differently when we've begun to engage in something. This is why cliffhangers are used on our favorite TV shows. Our brain remembers the last episode because it was interrupted, and it wants a conclusion.[16] Likewise, just getting started diffuses the other brain trickery—the overestimation of how difficult a task will be. How many times have you started on something and wound up telling yourself, "This ain't so bad"?

The key here is to stop waiting for the magic "I feel like it" moment. Odds are it won't come. As researcher Pychyl puts it, "Procrastinators delay a task because they are not in the mood to do it and deceive themselves into thinking they will be later on. When that time comes and they're not, they're in the same emotional place but with less time until the deadline."[17]

Whoops.

So let the power of "Just get going!" get you going.

- *Start with extremes*—First, break the task into a series of steps, including a number of small, measurable steps and ranging up to the most difficult steps. Then, start on either end. Do the worst first, or peel off a few of the super easy tasks right at the onset to start building momentum. A case can be made for either starting point—it depends on your preference.

  Getting the stressful worst part done first allows you to be more present with each of the tasks thereafter, rather than having that toughest task continually gnawing at you in the back of your mind. Your energy is highest at the start as well, thus increasing the likelihood you'll blast through the arduous task.

Starting with the easiest tasks feeds into our natural desire for instant gratification and can get the ball rolling.

- *Sync with your body's secret natural rhythm*—Beating procrastination means working smarter. And there may be no smarter way to work than in rhythm with your body's natural energy cycle (other than just making your intern do the work).

    Research by the U.S. Army revealed that our body and mind respond best to long periods of work (up to ninety minutes), followed by short breaks (fifteen minutes).[18] The Federal Aviation Administration discovered the same in a study that showed following this approach improved awareness and focus among pilots by 16 percent.[19]

    A method called the Pomodoro Technique encourages you to commit to this practice by setting a kitchen timer for 25 minutes of uninterrupted work, followed by a quick break.[20] So choose a length of time (whether it's 25 minutes, 90 minutes, or anywhere in-between), and get to work. You need to tap into all the natural energy you can to power through procrastination.

HOW TO STOP BEING A PERFECTIONIST

The only love procrastination gets is from the perfectionist, who employs it as a go-to tactic to delay starting that which they cannot completely dominate at that moment. This perfectionist is really a mutant, unhealthy alter-you. I find it quite helpful to personify my inner perfectionist, then put it in its place with some joyful aggression. You can too. Let it all out with these six insults.

Six Helpful Insults to Hurl at Your Inner Perfectionist

1. *"I'm gonna slap the 'should' out of you."* Seriously, strike the word *should* from your vocabulary. When perfectionists use the word, like in the sentences, "I should go over this again to make sure it's 100 percent right," "This should be a lot better than it is right now," or "I should have done X and Y," it's like granting a license for perpetual revisiting and remorse. Stop. Will more massaging really change the outcome? Tell yourself done is done, dammit.

2. *"Your perfectionism isn't just hurting you, jackass."* The collateral damage of your perfectionism is everywhere—don't underestimate it. Perfectionists tend to judge and criticize not only themselves but everyone else. The more they see their own flaws in others, the more they pick, as a sort of displacement mechanism. The constant criticism and judging isolates and distances the perfectionist from others, further exacerbating their "I must not be good enough" belief.

Perfectionists are often unaware of the impact this corrosive behavior has on others. They're assuming that everyone else is harshly judging them, so to do so as well is just the way of the world.

Expand your worldview and understand that your misplaced heat, like that of global warming, is indeed affecting the world around you for the worse.

3. *"Accept yourself before you wreck yourself!"* I had a friend who was a "textbook perfectionist" but reading between her lines didn't take much. Her perfectionism was a shield to protect her from any potential rejection, disappointment, or criticism. She was afraid everyone would see her for who she was, flaws and all, and that she just wouldn't stack up to their expectations. She was a prisoner to her perfectionism, and as I got to know her better and better I came to realize what she really longed for was love and affirmation, like we all do.

She broke free after a lot of introspection and after realizing, as in the prior point, that she was hurting more than just herself. The key to her exoneration was that she learned to forgive herself. She came to have the courage to be imperfect, began to appreciate that she was worthy of love and belonging, and learned to live with vulnerability and to stop controlling and predicting—a prescription in line with the teachings of noted vulnerability expert Brené Brown.[21] Brown teaches that we're all imperfect and wired for struggle.

Yes, even you.

4. *"How about less attitude and more gratitude?"* For me, my magic elixir for kicking the inner perfectionist in the groin is to practice gratitude. I've found that appreciating all I've done, versus obsessing over what I haven't, sets me free. And when I see in others all that they've become, rather than just seeing what they still need to be, my relationships with those people blossom. I'm more drawn to them and vice versa, and the deeper connection invites authenticity in—warts and all.

5. *"Get good at good enough for God's sake!"* The majority of the time, the odds are pretty good that no one is holding you to the same standards that you're holding yourself to. So how about we make like limbo and lower the bar a little? (Which was also the only way I could hit my numbers in the corporate world.)

The key to helping you do this? Realize that your goals are guides, not absolutes, and that they don't represent your worth.[22] It's important to discern the difference between healthy striving and dysfunctional perfectionism. There's nothing wrong with keeping high standards, of course—it's healthy to do so. The problem arises when we view success as "all or nothing," all the time.

Learning to delegate and let go is also helpful, as it reduces the temptation to engage in inspection, the security blanket for your inner perfectionist.

6. *"Stop being such a Catastrophic Cathy!"* Perfectionism can be fed by catastrophizing, or massively overestimating the negative impact of miscues or imperfections. We all know doomsday analysts like this, and also know how positively draining this negative outlook can be. Pay attention to your self-dialogue, and when you catch yourself drifting into this dark space, yank yourself back out into a lighter, more optimistic outlook. Keep in mind one of my favorite Twain quotes, "I've suffered a great many catastrophes in my life. Most of them never happened."[23]

HOW TO MASTER THE ART OF PUSHBACK

The Anti-Muse of Inundation has a way of piling it on us by preying on a weakness—the fact that it's neither fun nor easy to push back on those with authority/influence to create work. But while it may feel like a win to say "yes" in the near term, it will lead to losing in the long term.

The truth is, the path to least resistance will likely end in being overwhelmed, and an underwhelming sense of inspiration. The promising news is that by speaking up and pushing back, you can actually increase the chances of success in your career and for your organization, and earn more confidence and respect (not less)—even if it exposes you to a bit of potential criticism. Here's how to facilitate more of the former and less of the latter.

Four Ways to Push Back and Look Good Doing It

1. *Come from a place of accountability.* A legitimate reason for not taking on more work is if it unfavorably impacts current work. Requesters of work rarely have the visibility and awareness of the extent of your workload that you do. They'll assume everything is additive until you educate them otherwise.

Do so by visualizing your workload on paper, indicating how much work you think you can handle at any one point in time, explaining where your time is being spent (leaving out the part about team lunches at the casino), and then showing what other work would suffer. In this way, you can come from the high road of feeling accountable and acting responsible for the current work. No one can begrudge you that. You can still exude positivity and excitement for the total portfolio of work, including the new work, as long as adjustments can be made to the current workload.

By the way, as you raise awareness of your workload, include your "No Fly Zones"—time periods or projects that simply cannot be interrupted with competing priorities. These should be rare in occurrence but resolute in stature.

Armed with all of this, it's time to engage in mutual prioritization with the work requester—a partnership in making the best choices. (If it's your boss, also see the "Run your manager through the mill" section earlier in the chapter). Your tone throughout should be that of a respectful realist, not a roadblock.

2. *Give a different "yes" to requests.* "Just Say No" may have once worked as a big anti-drug campaign, but it often doesn't work in pushing back against requests. While you should be firm in your "no" and not water it down to avoid conflict, it's not a "no" in a vacuum.

You can say "yes" in spirit in different ways. Ensure that you understand the intent of the request, then strive to have empathy, present an alternate solution, or show support in some way. Again, this is not about waffling and ending up saying "yes" in a roundabout way to curry favor when you really meant to say "no." It's about leaving the pushback discussion with an aura of positive energy. Strategically stall in the face of the request if necessary, to avoid rushing to the more comfortable "yes" and to buy yourself time to frame your response in an energy-yielding manner.

Along the way, be careful of the pushback no-no's. Never just say "I don't have the time," because nobody does. Never say "you"; say "we." Although note that saying things like "*We* are driving me crazy with your stupid requests" probably takes this in the wrong spirit.

Anyway, to continue with the no-no's, let facts drive the discussion, never emotions. If the request for work is tied to a specific point of view that you disagree with, try pushing back on the point of view versus the person (which takes the emotion out of it). And when you do so, don't argue for your position, advocate for it.

3. *Use the Bermuda Triangle of Bargaining.* There are three variables to anything you're asked to do—time, resources, and scope. These three points form a devious triangle, into which effort can quickly and mysteriously disappear if the proper balance across all three isn't in place.

A fair and effective way to push back is to negotiate for variances. You can do the full scope of that new project with the agreed-upon resources, as long as you get twice the amount of time. Or you can meet that deadline and budget, as long as the scope of what's requested is scaled back. You get the idea.

4. *Treat "urgent" with kid gloves.* Urgent requests fall into their own category of consideration for their disproportionate contribution to disruption and inundation (and palpitations). Such requests are often accompanied with emotion and trickle-down pressure. Your boss feels it, so you will too. Feels like it might not be a good time to push back. As such, it requires a delicate touch, with special attention to the *intent, source,* and *pattern* of the urgent requests.

First, it's critical to discern the intent because urgent requests are often just "pass-along" requests, absent of any thought. It may well be the request can be met in some other, less work-intensive way.

Next, it's important to discern the source. Is it a request from the boss's boss, or higher, with heat to it? You may just want to get into execution mode. If it's not so highly ordained, there may be time to validate the request's urgency. If the urgent requests are constant and come from your boss, it's time to spell out the ripple effect that attending to these requests has on other work (see point one on this list).

Finally, keep an eye out for patterns to the urgent requests. Do they always come up before a standing, big quarterly meeting? Do they always accompany a visit from someone in the executive suite? If you discern a pattern, you can work to at least anticipate and flush out similar requests in the future. Ideally you eliminate the requests altogether with some advance planning, or at a minimum you downgrade the urgency from DEFCON 1, anyway.

HOW TO ASK FOR HELP

The Anti-Muse of Inundation wants you to shut your trap and suffer silently (like me with a "Honey-Do" list in hand). Often, you're all too happy to comply for fear of looking incompetent or being rejected. Besides that, research shows that self-reliance is one of our ten core values. But while self-reliance is admirable, it can also be self-limiting.[24] CEO of the LEGO Group, Jørgen Vig Knudstorp, takes it further by saying he believes that blame isn't for failure, it's for failing to ask for help. When you do ask for help, it can change everything.[25]

The truth is, asking for help is not a sign of weakness, it's a sign of wisdom. You just need a little wisdom in how to go about it, a few helping *HANDS*:

- *Have a specific ask*—Be able to articulate why you need help so you can pinpoint what help you need. Then, be specific in what you ask for as it will produce a more beneficial reaction. Research among panhandlers bears this point out. In one test cell the panhandler simply asked for money, with 22 percent of people complying and giving an average of $0.50 each. In the next scenario, the panhandler specifically asked for $0.37, and 36 percent of people complied—a better financial outcome. The study showed that when we give specific asks, it gives people the concrete criteria against which to decide if they want to help or not. Such asks are more likely to be acted upon because it's clear what can be done to help.[26]

• *Ask for advice versus help*—An effective way to ease the unease of asking is to turn it into an exercise of seeking advice.

Research from the Harvard Business School and the Wharton School indicates that advice-seeking is a different, easier bridge to getting help. This is because you're seeking information to inform a course of action, retaining control over the decision-making process, and flattering the other person by indicating that you value their knowledge and experience.[27]

• *Never ask timidly*—When we do muster up the courage to ask, we often still do so with trepidation, for fear that we're putting the other person out and that we'll get rejected (or because we just had garlic chicken for lunch).

However, research indicates that our fears are most often unfounded. The truth is, we vastly underestimate just how willing others are to lend a helping hand.

Researchers from Columbia University asked test participants to ask a stranger to borrow a cell phone or ask for an escort to a gym they couldn't find. Those who did indeed ask for help underestimated by as much as 50 percent how likely the other person would be to help.

It turns out that we also underestimate the social cost (feeling embarrassed) that others experience if they say no to our request for help.[28]

This is why I always ask to borrow money from an audience member while I'm on stage during a keynote.

Anyway, ask away, and when you do, do so with confidence. It will make the other person even more likely to want to invest what it takes to help you.

• *Do your due diligence*—It's one thing to help the truly helpless, but quite another when you are approached by someone being helpless. Don't be that guy/girl.

Make yourself helpable by showing up prepared, with a specific ask (as mentioned earlier), and even with options. Be sure that you've exhausted what you can do on your own. Be ready to share what's been tried and why it didn't work, why you feel that the person you're asking for help is the right one, and what you'll do with help if given. Finally, think through how the request for help could be a mutual win.

• *Start with a foundation of being helpful*—First, it's much easier to ask for help when you know you're a helpful person. Beyond that, being helpful triggers human nature and a desire for reciprocity.

Neuroscience research shows that we are hard-wired to show reciprocity in three ways. First, directly; you helped me, I feel compelled to help you. The more people you help, the broader your base of future supporters. Second, indirectly, others feel compelled to help you based on your reputation of being helpful, even if they haven't received help from you directly. Third, pay-it-forward reciprocity, where people simply want to help others because they themselves have been helped by someone else in the past.[29]

All in all, being a helpful person is just the right thing to do, but it also triggers a virtuous cycle of reciprocity.

You're never too busy to put the Anti-Muse of Inundation in her place.

Don't let the exhilarating sense of progress and feelings of preparedness be sidetracked. Don't let the opportunity to experience a sense of inspiration be drowned out by feelings of being overwhelmed.

You now have what you need in this chapter to fight back.

Sorry Inundation, we're gettin' busy on busting your agenda.

5

Loss of Control

(REVERTED)

EMILY, AN EXECUTIVE in a midsize company on the West Coast, could barely contain herself as she told me the story, chortles of laughter bursting from the seams of what she'd intended to be a brisk, professional telling.

She saw her boss, let's call her Elle Diablo, rushing through the vast cubicle farm that was Emily's existence, making a beeline for Emily's pod (which she time-shared with an Elvis-shaped carpet stain and the faint odor of her cube neighbor's feet).

"Emily!" shouted the Horned One.

"We just got the week's sales numbers—we're down again and Carlos will be here tomorrow to declare a full-blown crisis. I need to present your analysis on why we're declining so he can tell us what he wants to do—I don't want to look like a fool."

And then followed another gem, "I know you're meeting with some key accounts today about the declining sales but I need you to help me prepare for this meeting instead."

Emily interrupted her narrative to punctuate for me—"Can you believe she actually said all of this?"

Yes, Emily.

Yes, I can.

Going back to her story then, Emily told me she responded back to her boss immediately with her usual "You got it" response as her boss whirled and left as fast as she'd arrived.

She reiterated her boss's exact words to me (she wrote them down so she could later commiserate with coworkers): "I need to present *your* analysis on why we're declining so *he* can *tell us* what he wants to do—*I* don't want to look like a fool."

Three disempowering blows in one sentence that summed up the pattern that Emily's work life had fallen into. No sense of ownership or control in crisis, no seat at the table despite her being closest to the potential solution, and working off someone else's agenda as usual. Followed by an out-of-touch command to stop actually working *on* the problem and instead spend time on crafting a self-preserving story *about* the problem.

And that was the moment Emily told me she saw her last wisp of inspiration willingly impale itself on her letter opener.

Emily knew she wasn't doing anything to help the completely disempowering environment she found herself in. She had fallen into a pattern of her own of checking out, pleasing versus pushing back, openly spreading negativity, spiraling down at the slightest bit of feedback, and becoming far too numbingly reactive.

All behaviors that are entirely natural when the Loss of Control Anti-Muse is on the scene.

Inspiration and all that comes with it has no chance in such a soul-sucking soup. Even basic job satisfaction can't survive this toxicity. Studies have repeatedly shown that the single most important determinant of job satisfaction is working with a sense of control and autonomy—the degree to which employees feel they can make their own decisions and influence what happens on the job.[1]

But all, in fact, is not out of your control.

I walked Emily through a model I've developed to help many others regain a sense of control and autonomy, and now I'd like to share it with you.

It's all about deconstructing exactly how power flows in the phenomenon of self-empowerment, and then favorably influencing the ebbs and flows of this power.

By the way, since Emily put into practice what I'm about to share, she got promoted and has fallen in love with her job again, foot odor and all. She now counts herself inspired, while her former boss perspired her way right out of her job.

The one Emily now occupies.

May her ex-boss and this particular Anti-Muse both be ground into the great carpet stain of life.

And now it's your turn.

Let's break self-empowerment down so you can build it back up (Figure 5-1).

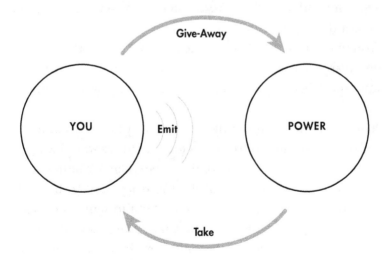

FIGURE 5-1
THE FLOW OF POWER IN SELF-EMPOWERMENT.

HOW YOU GIVE AWAY YOUR POWER

Whether or not we realize it, we take actions that directly give away our power. This is an awareness and avoidance campaign. Become aware of how you are doing this, and then avoid doing it. Here are the three most debilitating ways we give away our power and how to stop them:

1. *Your people-pleasing habit.* The truth is, while you're admirably giving of yourself with your people-pleasing tendencies, you're giving away more than you realize.

You sacrifice the power of bringing the authentic you to the table. To please others and gain approval, you say "yes" when inside you're screaming "hell, no," you tell bold-faced white lies to avoid hurting feelings, and you suppress your voice, the power of your words, and the value of sharing what you're really thinking. You do whatever you can to avoid confrontation, thus giving away the opportunity to change a situation for the better and to learn and grow from the change. You're giving away your personal productivity as you take on more and more in your desire not to disappoint and to be liked. You're acting like a robotic version of you, not the real version of you.

You may not realize that people pleasing quite often backfires. The pleaser acts as such to gain affirmation and instead draws contempt. Psychologist Maria Sirota explains this phenomenon:

> Human beings are highly sensitive to power dynamics in relationships, and we're always looking to see who the alpha is and who's at the bottom of the totem pole. We admire and reward those who are confident and we want to be their friend, marry them, and promote them to senior positions in our companies. On the other hand, we're aware, even if only on a subconscious level, of those who are insecure and lacking in confidence. People who aim to please come

across as weak and needy, and many of us are inclined to react negatively toward them.[2]

It gets worse.

Unfortunately, people pleasers attract manipulators who will take advantage of them, and they can even be the target of abuse from workplace bullies. In fact, it's estimated that 12 million people experience workplace bullying in some form each year, with people pleasers being the clear majority of those who report such bullying.[3]

So how do you shift the emphasis from pleasing to empowering? Try this bullet-point list to put a bullet in your bad tendencies:

- *Commit to 90 percent self-worth, 10 percent assigned-worth*— How you feel about yourself should flow dominantly from your own self-appreciation and self-acceptance—two things you must get better at.

  As a recovering people-pleaser myself, I know that's easy enough for me to say. And I know the purists might not agree with me on allotting 10 percent for external validation, but I'm a realist. Becoming completely callous to the occasional signal that you're valued for who you are and what you do is unrealistic. We all need that from time to time, and it's OK to seek it as a spirit-lifter and sense of accomplishment boost, as long as it's validation in response to the valid you. Or validation from an ex-flame who dumped you, that's pretty sweet too according to the Book of Adele.

- *Think of the You-niverse, not the universe*—Stop trying to be everything for everybody in the world (leave that to Ryan Seacrest). Start with you and ensure that you've set healthy boundaries that allow you to take care of your needs. Period. It will enable you to stay balanced, charged, and able to better serve others in a more authentic way.

Ask yourself if continually making others happy is really worth sacrificing your own happiness. It doesn't mean you've suddenly become selfish. People-pleasing behavior itself is actually selfish because you're doing what's easiest and are cheating others out of the benefit of your real thoughts and reactions.

- *Spot the difference between compassion and compulsion*—I'm not saying you can no longer act out of kindness and compassion (that behavior is reserved for the media). Just be on alert to what you're feeling when you choose to respond in a people-pleasing way. Are you doing it out of kindness? Great. As long as it's in balance with the You-niverse. Are you feeling compelled to do it to because you want to avoid conflict or want approval, and afterwards notice you feel ticked off that you gave in? Not great.

- *Remember that politicians never get 100 percent of the vote, and neither will you*—Not everyone will like you. It's a fact of life, and it's OK. So stop trying to make it so. I once asked a local politician friend how he dealt with knowing he got elected with only 51 percent of the vote. He responded, "I put myself out there knowing not everyone will agree, especially in this business. I don't take the 49 percent as personal, I take it as perspective."

  Odds are you're getting much more than 51 percent of the vote by the way, and for those few who don't get you, take it in perspective. The world's a big place with an infinite number of chemical compositions. A few of the blends are bound to be combustible.

- *Break the mirror (it won't lead to bad luck)*—People pleasers tend to act like a mirror that just reflects back the person they're in front of at the time. Think of this mirror metaphor when you catch yourself in pleasing mode and giving away your personal power, and shatter it. Replace the surface-level reflection with a deeper and more authentic representation—you.

And by the way, wouldn't you rather be liked as the real you, not some distorted funhouse-mirror version of you?

- *Push through unease to unearth growth and change*—It's not easy to press through the discomfort of saying "no," pushing back, or saying what's on your mind instead of what you think others want to hear. But in doing so you can change someone's point of view or help them realize something about themselves, to name just two outcomes. And don't discount the change you'll see in yourself as you become more assertive.

- *It came from somewhere, so send it back*—Odds are pretty good that you can trace the roots of your people-pleasing behavior.

  Perhaps it was an overbearing father, a scarring episode of rejection as a child, or an addiction to approval fed by an "everyone gets a trophy" culture. Lay on your own psychiatrist's couch and probe. Identifying the likely source allows you to stop beating yourself up for a moment and externalizes the pattern. It produces the "So why do I still do that?" effect and helps you start disassociating with the behavior.

  Once you think you've got the root cause nailed, personify it and let it know that it has become outdated, that you've decided to go a different direction, and that its services are no longer required. Give it severance pay if that makes you feel better.

2. *Playing the victim.* We've all played the part. No, I don't mean the teapot in the third-grade play.

I'm talking about feeling and acting like a victim when we're wronged, the next way we give away our power. It's part of our natural defense system. It's about the circumstances, not the self, so we place blame elsewhere and avoid responsibility. We might take slights as major offenses, feel someone is out to get us, be overly negative, see things as unfair, or have a "woe-is-me attitude" and seek out a sympathetic ear.

The problem arises when we fall into a pattern of such behaviors, which often occurs unbeknownst to us.

But you can bet that your friends, family, and coworkers know.

Playing the victim is the most devastating form of disempowerment because the core underlying belief is "I'm powerless."

Is there a better way to give away your power than to believe that you don't have any? (Other than getting married, I mean.) This leads to a learned helplessness and avoidance of action.

And worse yet, it's something you do to yourself. Country music star Naomi Judd said it best: "You only get to be a victim once. After that, you're a volunteer"[4] (said within the context of her battle with Hepatitis C).

If you suspect you're voluntarily giving your power away by playing the victim too often, then psychologist Leslie Becker-Phelps has a question for you.

Do you just want it to change? Or, do *you* want to change it?[5]

The former is how a victim thinks; the latter indicates you're ready to make your victim mentality a victim.

Here's how you do that—step by step.

- *First Step: Set Your Alarm*—It's easy to fall into victimhood and not realize it, so create a number of self-alerts to catch it early on. Really pay attention to when you start to complain, blame, go negative, or exaggerate about an unfavorable outcome. When in a victim mentality, your mind is set—but you must change your mindset. That starts with putting signal flares in place for when you're slipping into old habits.
- *Second Step: Give Your Rescuers Resolve*—Those trapped in a victim mentality often have a core group of "rescuers" they turn to for sympathy. The well-meaning audience

often feeds the victim mentality by showing pity and even commiserating.

Redirect your first-responder unit by asking them not to feed your downtrodden behavior. This can be a very difficult step because it requires brutal self-honesty and vulnerability.

Do it anyway.

- *Third Step: Pinpoint Your Part in It*—When something happens for which you feel victimized, before you start the blame game, ask yourself, "What was my role in this? How might I have contributed?" Be honest. Instead of using "You" or "They" in your reactions, use "I." Own your part of the story before you move on to the Fourth Step.

- *Fourth Step: Edit Your Stories Before You Tell Them*—I don't get to just tell you my stories straight up. I first turn them in to my editor, who always helps make them better (and who patiently converts them from crayon into Microsoft Word).

   Do your stories focus on problems and end up holding you back, versus focusing on solutions and moving you forward? Do you tell stories underscored with tones of pity and resentment, seeking sympathy? Do you perpetuate your story, making your thing everything, even though we all have our thing?

   Similar to the First Step, the point is to catch yourself as you start to tell a story, pause, and then turn it in to your internal editor for some rewrites if necessary. Try this trick—when you catch yourself starting a story with a "This is a wayward thing" tone, switch to a more accepting "This is the way of things" tone.

- *Fifth Step: Channel Your Inner Hippie*—Gratitude, forgiveness, and peace, baby. You need it all to get out of victimhood. Do right by not homing in on how you were wronged. Instead, think of all the ways you've been blessed in your life. Forgive those who have trespassed against you—odds are they're worthy of your forgiveness. Don't add to the drama—we have enough in this world (I'm looking at you, celebrity marriages). Find peace, not pain.

- *Final Step: Take Charge, Dammit*—I'm not swearing at you, I'm swearing with you, because this takes resolve. Playing the victim can be comforting. You can feel exonerated, validated, and free from having to take action and risk (because you're powerless after all).

  Taking charge is none of that—but it's required if you want to replace self-incarceration with self-inspiration. Commit to taking responsibility for your work, for your life, and for the attitude, actions, beliefs, and behaviors that fuel all of it. We'll talk more on how you can take power back in a bit.

3. *Disempowering Self-Dialogue.* The last debilitating way in which we give away our power is when our inner monologue turns on us, like a drunk hockey fan on ten-cent beer night.

We ask ourselves disempowering questions like "Why can't I catch a break?" "Why did I screw that up?" "Why did he get promoted instead of me?" "What's wrong with me?" "What if the hokey-pokey really *is* what it's all about?" and so on.

Anyway, we'll beat ourselves up incessantly and pummel ourselves with limiting thoughts, beliefs, and attitudes. We often don't realize we're doing it or if we do, we can't help ourselves.

It's like we can't give away our power fast enough.

So why do we do it?

I know what you're thinking, "Here comes the leather couch and psychotherapy."

That's not good enough for my readers. I'll do you one better. Hypnotherapy.

A study by *American Health* magazine has shown hypnotherapy to be two-and-a-half times more effective and 100 times faster at treating patients than psychotherapy.[6]

So to help you figure out why you engage in self-disparagement, dear reader, I enlisted the best: board certified hypnotist, instructor, author, speaker, and executive hypno-coach Lisa Zaccheo.

Zaccheo has treated thousands of patients with a wide range of ailments, all of whom engage in disempowering self-dialogue almost as a default. Whether their affliction is overeating, constant extramarital affairs, drinking too much, or extreme disappointment over not getting that promotion, they exacerbate the issue by verbally beating themselves up over it.

To change patients' inner monologue and address their problem head-on, Zaccheo first gets them to understand that their issue as they see it (overeating, etc.) is merely a symptom, and that they must come to grips with the root cause of the problem.

Amazingly enough, the root cause turns out to be the same for everyone she sees, regardless of their ailment.

Back to that in a moment.

To get to the root cause of any ailment, Zaccheo has to get past the conscious mind, because the conscious mind is merely the surface layer, the tip of the iceberg. It's rational and analytic and feels compelled to come up with a reason for why things are the way they are (even if it's not the *real* reason).

Below the conscious mind are stacked layers of fear that wreak havoc by burying our truth and producing unhelpful thought patterns that turn into beliefs. These beliefs motivate decisions and create emotions and habits that don't serve us well.

To get through all this noise, Zaccheo opens up conversation directly with her clients' subconscious, an able dance partner as it can process an astonishing 40 million bits of information per second and represents about 90 percent of our mental capacity. This is especially impressive when compared to that slacker called the conscious mind, which equates to about 10 percent of our mental capacity and phones it in at 40 bits of information per second.

Delving into the subconscious mind is pay dirt because it's where vast amounts of deeply buried information is stored. It's the place where all our emotions, habits, and patterns reside. The subconscious houses our long-term memories and knows where the origin of all our stuff, the good, the bad, and the ugly, is. It's where truth lives.

It's like the Oprah of our psyche.

As Zaccheo helps her variety of clients access the valuable information within the subconscious, working their way past the negative self-talk and through the layers upon layers of fear and limitation, something fascinating, even amazing, happens.

The same damning belief, the same root cause, in one form or another, keeps surfacing over, and over, and over again.

"I'm not good enough."

Sound familiar?

The crazy part is, Zaccheo says this belief is most often based on a misperception or a personal experience taken the wrong way. Zaccheo indicates that the belief has become an epidemic in the workplace; we beat ourselves up, project our "not good enough" onto others, and then they volley it right back. And everyone spirals down in a disempowering death spin.

The point is that the fundamental first step in stopping your disempowering self-dialogue is to stop telling yourself that you're not good enough.

As Zaccheo pleaded with me to share with you,

"Not good enough" comes from differences—we think our differences are a curse instead of a blessing. We think our differences make us lesser than, but they make us greater than. We simply must get in touch with "I'm good enough" and "I'm meant to make a unique contribution." You must believe that you are exceptional. You must believe you have the potential for *your* special kind of greatness, and that you're getting better each day.

OK. We're Good? Enough?

Let me close out this section by saying this. I had other well-researched wisdom to give you to help put an end to your disempowering self-dialogue. Suggestions about building positive affirmations into your life and ditching the negative Nellie personalities you associate with, talking to yourself like you would your best friend, not someone you don't like—that sort of stuff.

Instead, let me simply reiterate these crucial words from Zaccheo so you can focus on taking them to heart:

"We think our differences make us lesser than,

but they make us greater than."

HOW YOU CAN TAKE BACK A SENSE OF POWER

When working in a disempowering environment, we often feel compelled to concentrate on just surviving, let alone trying to figure out how to wrestle some sense of control back. But at some point, hopefully before the point of exhaustion and height of frustration, we simply must intervene on the pattern in place. Waiting it out rarely works if we want to feel inspired at work again anytime soon.

Research indicates that the problem in trying to regain some semblance of control lies in where to start.[7] The chaos can be all-encompassing and if initial attempts at effecting change fail, our resilience can quickly wear down.

This makes us more likely to submit to feelings of powerlessness, like when trying to reach an actual human being on a customer service number.

We lament over the situation we're in, wishing it were different and letting it eat at us. We wish we had more resilience and when we don't we spiral further down, like a narcoleptic at a tax law convention. We want to take action and regain a sense of control but we don't know how.

But there's hope. It turns out that the most effective starting point for taking back personal power is within your power.

It starts with letting go of what you can't control and homing in on what you can.

And doing so with an eye to better days versus bitter days.

Consider the remarkable story of Courtney Clark.

Clark was diagnosed with cancer, stage 2A invasive malignant melanoma, at the age of 26. Maintaining relationships can be extraordinarily difficult in such situations, and so Clark was also forced to add the title of divorcée to the unexpected ledger of her life.

She enjoyed three better years before cancer returned for a second time. This time around, because it was caught early, she was shaken more mentally than physically, her belief system uprooted. She told me she had been conditioned, like so many of us, to believe that our lives follow the path of a Hollywood movie. There's one major challenge in our lives, one wicked witch to vanquish, which we do, and then we continue our journey down the yellow brick road to an eventual happy ending.

But nobody gave Clark the script.

Five years later she was able to celebrate five years being cancer free, which is critical for cancer survivors as it's at that point that chances of recurrence go down and the survival rate goes up. Clark had a party with her friends, complete with a key lime pie and a candle in the shape of a 5. Feeling bullish, it was at that time that she and her doctor decided to get a baseline MRI head scan to ensure that all was good in the Land of Oz. Sure enough, the scan showed no cancer.

However, it did show a brain aneurism, unrelated to any cancer, that could rupture at any time and kill her if not operated upon.

Three brain surgeries later, including a craniotomy in which the top of her skull had to be removed, the aneurysm was treated.

At last, some respite for Clark and a chance to put a horrific stretch of health problems behind her as best she could.

Until cancer returned for a third time not long after, and was beaten back, yet again, by a determined, extraordinary woman.

Despite this incredibly unfair turn of events, and while Clark admitted to me she was on the edge of despair at moments, she never submitted to a sense of powerlessness.

How on earth is that possible?

Focus.

That is, Clark placing it squarely on *what she could control*, and getting absorbed in the details of it all.

And all while remaining future-focused, not survival-focused.

During the height of Clark's battle with her illnesses, she sought solace in controllable details like which hospital to go to, which doctor to see, how to pack for her extended hospital stays—all things she could have delegated but instead chose to take the reins on. Every detail she could own, she did. She stayed future-focused by breaking the unfathomably giant task of cancer treatment and brain surgery down into bite-sized pieces where she could exert control and envision an outcome.

Courtney Clark's approach is supported by research on torture survivors in South America. The few survivors who did not suffer from persistent post-traumatic stress syndrome reported success at maintaining some sense of personal control during their horrific ordeal. As the research indicated, "Some reported setting rules in their own minds, only screaming after having counted to a certain number, or eating food in a certain order of their choosing. They were still doing some things on their *own terms*."[8]

As of this writing, Clark was one-year cancer free and as focused as ever—this time on building her budding career as a content-based motivational speaker and author.

While Clark's story is inspiring enough, just as inspiring is the fact that you too can have remarkable resilience and take back a sense of control and personal power. That's because it doesn't matter if you're naturally resilient or not, naturally optimistic or not. No matter what you face, it's within your power to focus on what you can control and what the future could hold.

What follows is a tool that will help you direct your focus in such endeavors.

To set it up, we zap over to the world of electricity, where within lies a central player known as a power grid. The power grid is the system of power plants, transformers, and wires that carries electricity across the land (all in an effort to keep your eighteen devices charged).

Here, the power grid is a tool based on research among over 1,000 executives that lists the ten most potent actions *within your control* to help take back a sense of control and personal power.[9] While you'll never be able to have a sense of control with everything, these tactics are a proven way to build a reenergizing foundation. Start with a few tactics listed in Table 5-1., then work in more as you steadily expand your sense of empowerment and control.

TABLE 5-1
THE POWER GRID

SELF-EMPOWERMENT TACTICS	POWER NOTES
1. Get Off Others' Agenda and On to Your Own.	This doesn't mean being insubordinate. It involves stepping back and figuring out what you want, setting a path, and setting concrete goals that matter. The goals should have significance and meaning to you so they *compel you to take action* and so that holding yourself accountable to them is deeply personal.
2. Be an Expansion Zealot—of Mind, Experiences, and Connections.	Self-empowerment is directly correlated with your commitment to broadening your perspective. Expand your mind by holding the commitment to learn new things sacred. Expand your worldview by trying new experiences and seeing the gift in each one. Expand your network by reaching out and making new connections.

SELF-EMPOWERMENT TACTICS	POWER NOTES
3. Reconfirm and Reapply the Real You.	It's easy to lose sight of our authentic selves when we keep seeing our sense of control slip away. Be intentional and take a pause to check in with yourself—what are your core beliefs, values, and preferred attitudes and how are you showing up relative to them? Is your unique voice fading, blending in with external opinions? Do you need to get back to being who you truly are? Are you flexing your natural strengths? There may be no purer, more sustainable power source than when you get back to excelling at being you.
4. Balance Solo-Powered with Solar-Powered.	Counterintuitively, self-empowerment doesn't just come from depending on yourself. It also comes from taking in the "solar energy" around you—the brightness and wisdom of others willing to share, the people eager to help, the optimism and support oozing from friends. Don't try to do it all alone, draw power from others willing to give it to you. This includes establishing your Personal Board of Directors. Seek out a group of trusted mentors to help give you the guidance and soul checks you're missing today.
5. Push for Role Clarity.	One of the more helpless feelings in existence is that of not knowing what you're really supposed to be doing or how you fit into the puzzle. Don't let your chain of command off the hook. Push for clarity on what your role is and how you fit into the bigger picture.
6. Take a Seat at the Decision-Making Table.	This is more doable than you think. The best insight for doing this comes from functions within a company that are all too often treated as "peripheral." Functions like Design, HR, and PR often have to work hard at getting a voice in molding decisions. Here's how they do it: • Come with data and speak to it without fear. • Know your competitors, industry trends, and end user better than anyone else. Know history (historians get invited to the table). • Understand your business model, strategies, and how success is measured (to be able to "play up" to the level of the higher-ranking). • Be a willing change agent, accountable, solutions/action/results oriented, and the CEO of your projects (breathe mastery).
7. Stop Asking for Permission.	Make the call. Assume the role. Just go for it. You'll learn where the boundaries are. Home builders need a permit for everything—business builders don't.

continued . . .

SELF-EMPOWERMENT TACTICS	POWER NOTES
8. Thrive on Feedback.	You take back some control when you control how you react to feedback. Think of feedback as a GPS for your goals. If you get off course and that pleasant electronic voice kicks in to redirect you, do you react negatively? Of course not, you're thankful for the redirect. Think of feedback the same way. It's intended to help get you where you want to go. Recalculating . . . Destination Betterment!
9. Embrace Change, Energetically.	Let others wilt in the face of change. You can grow stronger and more in control through change, ironically. The key lies in how you direct your attitude and energy. View anxiety as anticipation. Put your energy into the new beginning in front of you, and gracefully leave behind what can no longer be. While you're at it, don't just glorify the past, open your mind to how it may have been burdening you as well. Take the opportunity to reevaluate not only the past, but the present and future as well. Spend less time fighting the change, more time forming it to fit a desired end-goal. Realize that there can be no change without discomfort, nor can there be any real growth without discomfort either. And give the benefits of change time to flourish.
10. Develop the Proactivity Muscle.	Being proactive puts power back in your hands. Of course, it's easy to say "Be more proactive!" It's harder to develop the tendency. To get the most bang for the buck on this front, think EAGER: **E**volve your predictive ability. Learn to anticipate issues and events by identifying patterns and taking time to scenario plan. **A**lways add value. Make it a mantra. Revel in your resourcefulness in so doing. Taking this approach forces proactivity as passivity can't deliver up to this standard. **G**et off the sidelines and participate. Develop a discomfort with not being in the mix. **E**stablish a habit of over-communicating. You take more control by doing this and get more back as it encourages reciprocation. **R**ustle the snakes out of the grass. Commit time to look for, spot, and fix problems before they bite you.

HOW YOU EMIT POWER

You already intuitively know how you emit power (beyond just good hair days). You do so when you act with full engagement, energy, positivity, and self-confidence. In so doing, others are drawn to your efforts and want to participate and emulate. Thus, you yield empowerment as a by-product of your actions.

In fact, acting with self-confidence is so important that we'll tackle that separately in Chapter 6, "Dwindling Self-Belief (Revitalized)," as part of an overall plan to strengthen your personal presence and inner fortitude—foundational requirements for inspiration to take hold.

For this section, however, it's important to cover three often overlooked ways you can embody, and in return attract, a greater sense of control and personal power:

1. *Share your gifts in servitude.* This one's short and sweet. People are drawn to your efforts to be a force for good. They will see the energy you're putting into helping them and others and be appreciative of and influenced by it. They will want to pay it forward, thus having a multiplicative effect on the positive power you wield. Time and time again, you will experience the truth that power comes right back to you when you share yours (in the form of your time and unique talents).

2. *Emit the power of vulnerability.* Counterintuitively enough, when you're willing to show your weakness it's a sign of strength. A sense of authenticity radiates and draws people to you as you emotionally expose yourself. (Please note that physically exposing yourself will not draw the same reaction.)

Ask yourself, who are you more compelled by, a leader who stands on a stage and professes to have the answer for everything, encasing it all in bravado, or the leader who admits their mistakes and indicates when they're asking for help?

No contest.

But it's never that easy, of course. As world-renowned vulnerability expert Brené Brown (whom I mentioned in the previous chapter) puts it, "The difficult thing is that vulnerability is the first thing I look for in you and the last thing I'm willing to show you. In you, it's courage and daring. In me, it's weakness."[10]

Resist the temptation to view vulnerability as a major blemish, one that necessitates masking (save that for your hickeys). Instead, embrace it, wear it like a badge of pride and revel in the fact that you will embolden others to show up the same way. You can't help but emit power when you're showing vulnerability because it comes from the very core of being human.

3. *Be in control during crisis.* A loss of control and the uninspiring feelings that go with it can go into overdrive in times of crisis. In my experience, leaders do one of three things in a crisis: shine, stumble, or crumble.

The ones who shine exude a low-thrumming, but constant, source of calm control that others rally around and draw inspiration from. You can be that leader or help that leader show up as such while modeling ideal, in-control behavior yourself.

I studied the worst to give you the best. No, not the Kardashians. Here are five lessons for how to be in control during crisis from some of the worst crises the United States has seen in recent memory: the Cuban Missile Crisis, September 11th, Hurricane Katrina, the anthrax attacks, and the BP oil spill. My hope is to pull something useful from devastation to give you inspiration.

Five Crisis Control Lessons from Some of America's Worst Crises

1. *Start with the 5 C's: Calm, Candor, Communication, Concern, and Courage (lessons from 9/11 and the anthrax attacks of 2001).* In the midst of the 9/11 crisis, New York City mayor Rudy Giuliani applied a lesson learned from his father. In the event of an emergency, always be the calmest person in the room. Giuliani's

approach gave a jittery America the sense that there was some control at hand, helping to allay fears as much as possible in an impossible and implausible situation.[11] Giuliani also excelled at providing frequent communication and candor (both intertwined with hope and reality)—core tenets of all leaders that exude control during crisis.

Empathizing and showing concern for the crisis at hand is also essential. Following the anthrax attacks of 2001, advisers to the Centers for Disease Control and Prevention (CDC) Office of Communications listed as a primary guideline the need to acknowledge uncertainty in a crisis. As chief adviser Peter Sandman put it: "When you're certain, say so. When you're almost certain, say that. And when you're feeling your way—which is inevitably going to be often—say that. And when you acknowledge uncertainty, show your distress and acknowledge your audience's distress: 'How I wish I could give you a definite answer on that....'"[12]

The last of the 5 C's may be the most important for actually resolving the crisis at hand—acting with courage. Rarely does taking small, incremental steps effect the change needed to reverse the situation at hand if it's truly a crisis.

2. *Get clear on reality (a lesson from the Cuban Missile Crisis)*. Being in control during crisis has as its foundation an understanding, and acceptance, of reality. Slow down and simplify the situation. In so doing, do not underestimate the size of the problem or the magnitude of steps you may have to take. Anticipate the worst-case scenario and get out ahead of it.

That said, cut through any confusion to clearly understand the reality in front of you so as not to underreact, or overreact.

Confusion, misunderstanding, and near overreaction almost threw the United States into a nuclear war with the Soviet Union during the Cuban Missile Crisis in October 1962. Throughout the crisis, there were many confusing and misunderstood events. None was more precarious than the events of October 27, dubbed "the most dangerous day in history." On this day, U.S.

ships discovered one of four Soviet submarines patrolling the coast of Cuba (submarines that, it would later be discovered, were armed with torpedoes tipped with Hiroshima-sized nuclear bombs). The Soviet submarine commanders were all cleared to fire at their discretion and, scarier still, had been out of communication with Moscow for weeks (given the depths they were patrolling at) with no understanding of what was happening on the surface above.

The aircraft carrier USS *Randolph* fired depth chargers near the Soviet subs as a signal that they needed to surface immediately, as they had informed Moscow they would do. The Soviet subs, being out of contact with Moscow, misinterpreted this act as one of extreme aggression. The two officers on board the Soviet submarine each consented to use their half of the torpedo launch key, and prepared to let all hell loose. The unthinkable was avoided only because the commander of the entire Soviet fleet, Vasilli Arkhipov, happened to be on board that same sub and told his officers, who had full rights to fire in absence of him, to stand down and buy time to clear up what was a confusing scenario. Thus, nuclear war was averted and Arkhipov came to be known as "The Man Who Saved the World."[13]

So, before you fire your own missiles, make sure you fully understand the situation.

3. *Create a unity of effort (a lesson from Hurricane Katrina).* Admiral Thad Allen of the U.S. Coast Guard is one of the most practiced leaders in crisis response of our times. Allen managed the New York Harbor during 9/11, and managed the responses to Hurricane Katrina and the BP oil spill in the Gulf of Mexico. The primary lesson Allen learned across all of these experiences was the need to clearly define and frame the problem in a manner that would get everyone on the same page and *unified in their efforts* to produce an agreed-upon outcome.

For example, when Allen arrived on the scene after a week of widely criticized initial response efforts to Katrina, he soon discovered that this was no ordinary hurricane in terms of its impact. Once the levees were breached and the city of New Orleans was flooded, the concept of a hurricane response no longer applied—a fact Allen says the nation was slow to understand.

He likened Katrina's effects to that of a weapon of mass destruction.

New Orleans had lost continuity of government and was unable to take in all the resources that were flowing in and redeploy them to where they were desperately needed. Once Allen moved rapidly to reframe the depth of the crisis and unify response efforts, it began the response turnaround for which Allen was so widely lauded.[14]

4. *Set a North Star, and the waypoints to get there (another lesson from Hurricane Katrina).* One of the first things Allen did upon his arrival at the Hurricane Katrina scene was to set a North Star—a big, bright goal that everyone could rally around. Such a thing was sorely needed among an exhausted, demoralized response team who were under intense pressure from a recovery effort being broadly criticized. Allen gave them only one order: to treat any storm victims they came across like they were their own family. As he tells it, "After I said that, … literally a cheer broke out. Because so many people were trying to figure out, because of the pressure that had been exerted on the response, and the perception that it wasn't going well, just a simple set of core values and a North Star to steer by I think is what they were looking for."[15]

With a North Star in place, it's also critical to put a detailed plan, procedures, and trusted team in place, to line up the resources (reallocating them if necessary), and to stay supremely flexible, as things may change.

5. *Be visible up the chain and on the front line (a lesson from the BP oil spill).* During the BP oil spill, Allen spent 50 percent of his time in Washington and 50 percent of his time out on the boats in the Gulf, in 110° heat index conditions.[16] He knew his credibility on both fronts depended on his being visible.

So establish who the hierarchy is that you'll need support from and stay visible to them, but never forget that the people in the trenches need to see you the most.

You can get a sense of control back by learning to control the flow of power in self-empowerment. Take personal power back, stop giving it away, and emit a sense of control such that it begets an even greater sense of control. Accordingly, inspiration will flow as well.

So what say we leave the Loss of Control Anti-Muse with a loss of control over us?

6

Dwindling Self-Belief

(REVITALIZED)

LOOK AT A globe and try to pinpoint the most isolated place on the planet.

There, standing by itself with nothing in sight, like me at my 8th grade dance, you'll find Hawaii.

Did you ever wonder how in the name of Beyoncé it was originally discovered, being hopelessly situated thousands of miles from any other land?

Ancient Polynesians pulled off this miraculous feat of exploration somewhere around 1100 A.D., long before the GPS and ocean vessels existed.[1]

But how?

It was the golden plover that first tipped them off.

The Polynesians, who inhabited the Marquesas Islands in the South Pacific, noticed that the bird, a land bird, annually left the islands and headed north over the ocean.[2]

Hmmm.

They decided to follow (cue chase music), certain that the bird would lead them to new lands. But the bird was fast, and each year the Polynesians could keep up for only so long, so they'd have to head back to try again the next year.

Out into the massive, frightening ocean they'd head year after year in their carved wooden sailing boats, with only the stars serving as a guide and map of their progress.

Of course, the Polynesians didn't know this, but Hawaii lay in the middle of what's now called the Polynesian Triangle (New Zealand, Easter Island, and Hawaii), which encases over 10 million square miles of ocean. Armed with today's knowledge, a direct course, and a modern sailing boat, it takes thirty days to travel the 2,500 miles to reach Hawaii from the Marquesas Islands.

This was a gnat in a haystack, not a needle.

But they had to believe, especially in themselves and their approach. The fortitude required for such a mission had to be astounding, particularly because estimates indicate that it took them *400 years* to find Hawaii using their methods.[3]

Only a strong sense of self-belief passed through generations could have kept them going and, just as important, kept them positive-minded enough to spot vital clues along the way, like the plover. Other little wisps of inspiration presented themselves en route to help as well.

The Polynesians noticed how the wave patterns changed near land mass, and could tell from changes in swells if the boat was still heading in the direction they intended. They picked up on debris floating in the water, especially vegetation, calculating how far from land the debris must be, based on known speeds at which it could travel in water and its level of deterioration. They noticed that the hue of clouds over land took on a different color based on reflections caught from the terrain.[4]

They ultimately succeeded in the face of an incredible task because they believed in their skills and had ironclad fortitude. Their inner strength kept them receptive to catching inspiration from the clues all around them.

When our inner strength dwindles we can feel adrift and alone in what becomes a seemingly massive ocean. This Anti-Muse revels in the fact that our downtrodden outlook will leave the inspiration all around us to just float by.

Such a powered-down state takes the form of low self-confidence, a lack of perseverance, a tendency to withdraw from the moment (not being fully and energetically present), and a sense of not being well-respected.

If this is where you're navigating, it's time to change course.

Know that you're not alone. For every story of Polynesian-like triumph there are a thousand stories of those who came close to discovering something wonderful (perhaps not knowing just how close) before they turned back.

Let's strengthen your inner strength to ensure that your story won't be included among the near-misses of self-discovery.

SELF-CONFIDENCE

It may surprise you just how important it is to have self-confidence.

An interesting study published by the *International Journal of Cosmetic Science* showed the impact that self-confidence can have on attractiveness.

In the study, a group of men were given a good-smelling cologne to wear while another group of men were not given a cologne. Both groups were then rated by a female panel on attractiveness (I never said this study was the height of profundity).

When the women were looking at photographs of the men, there was no difference between the groups of men in mean attractiveness ratings. However, when viewing video clips, the same panel of women judged men using the cologne as more attractive, suggesting a clear behavioral difference between the groups of men.[5]

A behavioral difference, that is, driven by a greater sense of (cologne-induced) self-confidence.

Similarly, a study by Webster University, conducted at a bar no less, found that a woman's best move for attracting men and getting asked out was a confident smile with a direct gaze.[6] I'm guessing the second-best move was for the woman to position herself such that... blocking the line of sight ESPN on the TV behind her.

Meanwhile, back at the workplace, the importance of self-confidence rears its head again. A study by the University of Melbourne showed that there's a correlation between advancement at work and self-confidence levels, even self-confidence levels dating back as early as primary school.[7] And confident workers tend to be happy, fulfilled, maximally productive workers who are motivated to achieve higher performance.[8]

This sense of self-efficacy also means you're more likely to notice and pull on threads of inspiration because you believe they'll lead you to a positive outcome of your own making. Relatedly, when you feel self-confident, you don't feel the need to bring anyone down— just the opposite in fact. Therefore, you're more likely to be working in a mutually supportive, inspiring environment.

Maximum self-confidence matters.

And yet the levels of self-confidence in the workplace are shockingly low, especially among women. In a recent survey conducted by the Institute of Leadership and Management, on average a full 40 percent of the workforce reported not having high self-confidence levels, with the split being 30 percent among men and a troubling 50 percent among women (and that's just on average—I'd argue 100 percent of both sexes experience substantive downward spikes in self-confidence at times).[9]

Katty Kay and Claire Shipman, authors of *The Confidence Code*, point out that despite the undeniable progress that women have made in the workforce on matters like holding leadership positions and fueling profitability (half a dozen global studies show that companies with a large female workforce outperform their competitors on every measure of profitability), there is still a large self-confidence gap between men and women. Kay and Shipman state: "Compared with men, women don't consider themselves as ready for promotions, they predict they'll do worse on tests, and they generally underestimate their abilities. This disparity stems from factors ranging from upbringing to biology. A growing body of evidence shows just how devastating this lack of confidence can be. Success, it turns out, correlates just as closely with confidence as it does with competence."[10]

What a travesty.

What follows is some gender-neutral advice to help you unfurl your wings. Let's cut the tether holding us down and release ourselves to soar.

Eleven Ways to Elevate Self-Confidence

1. *Shut down the nuclear reactor.* Self-confidence can plummet when we "go nuclear" with our fears and doubts and overreact to the actions of our boss and peers. Self-confidence problems are often triggered by our perception of what others' conduct says about us.

But there's a good chance their actions don't say anything about you—they're just actions. Be mindful in these instances and stop assuming the worst. Even if it's patently obvious their behaviors were intended to strike a blow to you, remember that no one defines you but yourself. As Eleanor Roosevelt said, "No one can make you feel inferior without your consent."[11]

2. *Mind the inner-monologue.* Our internal dialogue can either help or hurt us—don't let yours spiral downward. Recognize when this is happening and call it to a halt. In that moment, consider your self-talk as if you were an outsider. Change the tone like you would for a friend who needs support (or whom you want to borrow money from). And while you're at it, ask yourself "Why Me?" less and "Why Not Me?" more. The former is the victim mentality, the latter is the victor mentality.

3. *Go for authenticity, not approval.* When we seek approval we're seeking external validation, which is an empty victory at best, and elusive and confidence eroding at worst. Fall in love with your internal qualities, not external accomplishments. Internal validation is what counts and is as certain as your commitment to remain true to yourself, your values, and your beliefs. Self-confidence comes from self-congruency.

4. *Be prepared.* Leave it all on the field. Preparation breeds poise. As authors Linda Kaplan Thaler and Robin Koval wrote in *Grit to Great,* "When confidence becomes a muscle memory, panic is replaced by peak performance."[12]

Go so far as to engage in mental rehearsal. Sports psychologists have made an entire industry out of helping athletes to visualize their success.[13]

Taking action then and giving it everything you've got to actualize your goal (as mentioned in Chapter 2) is mission critical. When you don't it means a crisis of conviction, which is on the path to a crisis of confidence.

5. *Know that in the absence of confidence, courage takes over.*[14] That is, if you will it. And you must. Sorry to get all Yoda on you but you must face your fears and doubts. Quiet the voice that says "I can't" with deeds that say "I did."

6. *Self acceptance + self-responsibility = self-confidence.* You simply must accept your imperfections and take responsibility for your actions. The question isn't "who's to blame" but "what's to be done?"[15] Focus on potential, not limitations. Don't feel compelled to mask your mistakes; instead, view them as hard-earned progress toward an even better you. And resist the natural temptation to compare yourself to others that I also discussed in Chapter 2—compare only to your own personal code of conduct.

7. *There are always drops; it's how you pick up.* Human nature dictates the occasional crisis of confidence—for everyone. Yes, even The Rock. Probably. So know it when you're in it. Know that we've all been there. Know that the lows are necessary to experience higher highs. Then pull yourself out by pushing yourself up—into a more positive-minded direction. Draw on your memories of resilience to recover quickly and with authority.

8. *Don't validate parking.* Playing it safe all the time (parking) and not venturing out to try new things can you give the most temporary and false kind of confidence—one born out of simply avoiding failure. Become uncomfortable with long periods when you're not taking on new challenges. Successful new experiences breed self-confidence (even more than wearing that new cowboy hat). Draw on unswerving faith in your ability to figure things out along the way.

9. *Stop undermining yourself.* Self-deprecation is one thing, self-defamation is another. Don't lower others' expectations of you by doing it for them. Talking your self down (or excessively up) both smack of insecurity. Avoid making sweeping, negative generalizations about yourself from one isolated incident. You'd never want to make someone else who's extraordinary feel ordinary—why should it be any different for you? Stop the beat-down behaviors and engage in the lift-up behaviors.

10. *Create a safety zone.* If you're a manager, foster it; if you're an employee, ask for it. Make it safe to speak up, make it easy to ask for help, and make it comfortable to say "no." See failure as a complement to, not the counter of, success. Surround yourself with supportive people, not destructive. Stay focused on strengthening your strengths even as you admit and work on weaknesses. Be OK with being vulnerable.

11. *Respect, trust, empower, and praise.* Believe this as a boss, expect this as an employee. Treat respect and trust as non-negotiables, let them have the ideas and glory, and make praise commonplace. As Sam Walton, founder of Wal-Mart Stores, put it, "Nothing else can quite substitute for a few well-chosen, well-timed, sincere words of praise. They're absolutely free—and worth a fortune."[16] Followed by, "And note that Heinz ketchup is now on Rollback."

PERSEVERANCE

In Chapter 5, "Loss of Control (Reverted)," I talked about the importance of focus as a starting point for taking back a sense of control. Likewise, to persevere in pursuit of your goals, staying focused is critical. Focusing on completion of the job at hand despite the headwinds is job number one.

But when it comes to the art and science of persevering, focus alone isn't enough.

Why?

Because—and get ready for breaking news—persevering in the face of adversity can be *hard*. There's a reason why only 8 percent of us achieve our New Year's resolutions.[17] Other than the polar vortex, I mean, which, you know, screws us all up.

Anyway, it's time for a new story arc.

Literally.

To help you leap over obstacles and persevere follow this ARC—Awareness, Reframing, Coping (Figure 6-1).

FIGURE 6-1
THE ARC OF PERSEVERANCE

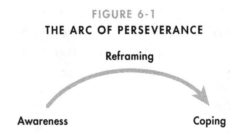

Reframing

Awareness   Coping

Awareness

There are several powerful truths to be keenly aware of as you face daunting challenges:

- *Know that persevering builds your skill set for the future—*
  Remembering this will help give you strength to carry on.

  Biographer Jim Tobin writes of how Franklin Delano Roosevelt handled his sudden onset of polio; it forged a skill set he'd apply to become one of the greatest leaders of the 20th century. He points out that the way Roosevelt used improvisation, experimentation, and perseverance in living with polio would ingrain skills that he directly applied to facing the challenges of the Great Depression and World War II. As Tobin wrote, "The way [Roosevelt] fought against his paralysis, trying one thing, then another when the first thing failed, and then a third, was perfectly reflected in his pragmatic response to the crises of his presidency."[18]

- *Know that developing mental toughness is a science-backed key to success—*In fact, research indicates that mental toughness is the *single most important factor* for success, even above intelligence (or having glossy teeth).

  A University of Pennsylvania researcher, Angela Duckworth, confirmed this in her study of West Point cadets. The first summer for the cadets includes a grueling series of dawn-to-midnight tests (known as the "Beast Barracks") intended to push the mental, physical, and emotional limits of the newbies. Duckworth found that those who survived the tests best were not the most gifted athletically or intelligence-wise. They were the ones with the most grit. In fact, cadets who were just one standard deviation higher on a test called the Grit Scale were *60 percent more likely* to finish Beast Barracks than their peers.

Duckworth confirmed the correlation between grit and success across many other professions, such as investment bankers, lawyers, doctors, painters, and journalists.[19]

You don't have to be a West Point enrollee or a Wall Street wonder to develop similar mental toughness. Nor is mental toughness based on a genetically predetermined mental condition. It's not a trait, it's a choice.

In fact, Duckworth's Grit Scale is based on two vectors: consistency of interest and perseverance of effort. Said another way, mental toughness comes from staying consistent in your drive to achieve a specific goal (not losing passionate interest in that goal) and then consistently putting in the effort to achieve that goal (using daily habits to help).[20]

Not genetics, grit.

- *Know just how debilitating worrying is*—The Anti-Muse of Dwindling Self-Belief loves to use worry as a bludgeon on those trying to persevere. We all worry from time to time. However, research indicates that it can quickly become a cycle of self-perpetuating negative thoughts that can hammer our likelihood to persevere. We move toward what we believe.[21] And this before you even get to the negative health consequences of excessive worrying.

  Science also bears solutions, though. Researchers at Penn State indicate the importance of identifying the object of worry, setting aside time to worry about it (no more than thirty minutes), and focusing on solutions during that time.[22] This is in contrast to the common belief that you should push your worries aside and keep plowing through when trying to persevere.

  In fact, research indicates that suppressing your worry altogether is an impossible task and that those who try to do so end up even more distressed.[23] (Jewish mothers everywhere can rejoice.)

  Net: Plan some time for productive worry, then don't worry about it.

Reframing

Perseverance can be massively aided by perspective. Here are three powerful ways to reframe your negative thought patterns when you need it most:

1. *When falling short, don't abandon ship.* Think of progress made. A fascinating dieting study by University of Toronto researchers indicates our tendency to give up when we know we're falling short.

Two groups of respondents, all on a diet, were asked to show up to a research facility without having eaten beforehand. They were then given a slice of pizza of the same size. One group was told their piece of pizza was larger than the other group's (even though it wasn't) in an attempt to make that group believe they had blown their dieting goals for the day. Both groups were then given cookies and asked to rate the cookies.

But the researchers weren't interested in their opinions on the cookies, they just wanted to see how many cookies each group of dieters would eat (like your judgy sister-in-law). The group that believed they had eaten the larger slice of pizza and thus had ruined their dieting goals for the day *ate over 50 percent more cookies.*[24]

This study indicates that when we miss an interim goal, we are much more likely to throw in the towel instead of instituting an acceptance and recovery mindset.

When faced with the realization that you've taken some missteps toward your goal, don't give up. Research indicates that the best way to handle this is to think of the progress you've made to date and know that all the positive steps that you've taken have moved you much farther forward than your misstep has moved you backward.[25]

2. *Personify your perseverance.* Sometimes we all need a friend to lean on. You can think of perseverance as a friend, a physical

entity to draw from so you don't feel like you're going it alone. Name it if you want. Call on it in times of need.

The Finnish actually have their own name for perseverance. They call it *Sisu*.

During World War II, the country of Finland was thrown into what became known as the Winter War with the Soviet Union. The Soviet Union deployed over 800,000 troops to the effort, 25 percent of Finland's entire population. By any estimate, the Finns seemed hopelessly outnumbered. Similarly, the 3,000 aircraft and 1,500 tanks used by the Soviet Union dwarfed the weaponry of the Finns, who had fewer than 100 operable planes and only 112 working anti-tank guns.[26]

That winter was particularly brutal as well, which is saying something for a country known for brutal winters. And in such circumstances, the typical eighteen hours of darkness that falls in the middle of winter must have seemed particularly ominous and spirit-sapping.

Things were bleak.

But despite all of this, the Finns had two advantages that would ultimately carry them to a standoff with the Soviet Union and the signing of the Treaty of Moscow on March 13, 1940.

First, the Finns' familiarity with rough winters and how to operate in them, as well as their knowledge of the Finnish terrain, were big assets.[27]

Second, the Finns drew on an old Finnish concept: Sisu.

As Sisu expert Emilia Lahti defines it: "*Sisu* is the concept of taking action in the face of significant adversity or challenge. It's not so much about achievement as it is about facing your challenges with valor and determination. *Sisu* provides the final empowering push, when we would otherwise hesitate to act."[28]

Kind of like getting encouragement from a friend when you need it most.

3. *Believe that you're right where you need to be.* Finally on the reframing front, you simply have to believe that the trials and tribulations you've faced are for a reason. Approaching challenges

with this mindset, that you're neither too far behind or ahead, gives you a sense of comfort and reminds you that it's all one step at a time.

Coping

As I said earlier, persevering is hard. Here's some battle-tested tactics to help you cope with difficulty along the way.

- *Remember the difference between perseverance and persistence—* We can persist doing things that might not even be good for us.[29] For example, we can keep dating someone we know isn't right for us or keep working at a job we hate. Or we can keep taking line-dancing lessons; I mean no-body wins there.

    My point is this.

    When we persist, the pursuit often *isn't worth it.*

    But when we persevere, the pursuit *is always worth it,* because *it's worthy.*

    It's worthy of our time, our sacrifices, and our passion.

    Again, as discussed earlier in this chapter, it's worthy as long as you remain passionate about the goal and the purpose behind it. Keep that worthy goal and purpose in front of you—it can be very easy to lose sight of it when things get difficult. Write it down or continually reiterate it to yourself.
- *Create a support network*—Enroll people you care about in what you're trying to accomplish. Lean on them when the chips are down. If whether or not you persevere af-fects others, think of it as healthy tension to help hold you accountable.
- *Remember you need self-discipline* and *self-compassion*—Anyone can tell you that you need self-discipline to persevere.

    But not everyone remembers that self-compassion is just as important.

Have tolerance and patience for your own learning process. When things go wrong, and they will, remember to take it easy on yourself.

- *See the humor and the honor in your pursuits*—Find humor in your struggles; it's certain to be there. You don't want to leave all the fun to circus carnies, after all. And recall that perseverance is a noble choice, something you can be proud of having exhibited.

- *Break things down and let science lift you up*—In Chapter 4, "Inundation (Relieved)," I shared "the Path Through Procrastination" and indicated the importance of starting with small steps. Similarly, perseverance can greatly benefit from breaking a big goal down into smaller goals and manageable pieces. You probably already know this and have experienced it several times.

  But what you might not know is that neuroscience is on your side when you do this. Researchers have discovered that when you achieve goals your brain releases little floods of a neurochemical called dopamine; this is what gives you that sensation of feeling good in the moment the goal is achieved. Thus, breaking a big goal into smaller goals gives your body more opportunities to experience that neurologically triggered good feeling. This is why dopamine is called the "reward molecule."[30]

  Seeking these little rewards via achievement of little goals can help you form new habits, ones that will help you persevere.

  This is why those seemingly mindless games you play on your mobile phone always seem to have a big goal broken into hundreds of little goals. The game-makers know you'll get a little rush with each goal achieved and thus you'll habitually keep playing (and paying in many cases).

  So perseverance doesn't have to be drudgery, it can be a series of physically and mentally pleasurable, confidence-building experiences.[31]

BEING PRESENT IN THE MOMENT

We've all been there—when you're there but you're not really *there*. You may be physically present but your mind and energy are elsewhere.

Believe me, people all around you notice.

And it happens far too often.

A Harvard study showed that our minds are not focused on what's in front of us a whopping 47 percent of the time, and in these times, our happiness level is at its lowest.

A wandering mind is not a happy mind.[32]

Babies have it figured out. Ever notice how charismatic babies are, how they seem to capture the room with their presence, without uttering a word? Psychologists will tell you it's not because of their magnetic personality, which isn't even fully formed yet. And set aside their cuteness, which is only part of it. It's because of how *present they are in the moment*, wide-eyed and fully engaged in everything that's right in front of them. There is something undeniably magnetic about someone who is giving 100 percent attention to what's in front of them in the here and now.[33]

It's no different for you—you too can be just as present.

Having a magnetic presence has an impact on others, the kind that will strengthen your belief that you're a conduit of positive influence.

When you're magnetically present you carry light with you everywhere you go. People are drawn to you, but, more important, their own unique energy is drawn out of them. You become a conduit for the pent-up expression of creativity, ideas, and thoughts that so many have buried inside them as they live days of transaction versus transcendence. The power of human connection kicks in and words, gestures, and facial expressions become emotional glue, not mere by-products of going through the motions.

Each encounter offers the opportunity to unlock greatness— *and inspiration.*

But, as with prizes at a raffle drawing, to win you must be present.

Now, admittedly, it's actually much easier to *not* be present.

And there are plenty of understandable distractions. Like kitten memes.

Anyway, with a little effort and intentionality, you can make your presence a present to those you interact with and help enable inspiration for all. Here's how.

Five Musts for Being Mindfully Present

1. *Accept that multi-tasking is a myth.* We sacrifice our power of full presence when we're multitasking. Forget for a moment that it can often be incredibly rude; we're not actually accomplishing what we think we are—we fool ourselves. The truth is that research indicates that multitaskers are actually *less* likely to be productive than those who focus on a single task, yet they feel more emotionally satisfied with their work, thus creating an illusion of productivity.[34]

In fact, research also shows that multitasking, or trying to do two cognitive things at the same time, simply can't be done—the mind doesn't work that way. Even trying to parallel path a cognitive activity with a more automatic activity doesn't really work; that's why the National Transportation Safety Board reports that texting while driving is the equivalent of driving with a blood alcohol level three times the legal limit.[35]

And many truly fool themselves, mistakenly believing that they're effective at multitasking, when in reality what they're good at is what researchers call task-switching.

Earl Miller, a professor of neuroscience at MIT, says that we simply can't focus on more than one thing at a time.

Period.

But what we can do is shift our focus from one thing to the next with astonishing speed. Says Miller, "Switching from task to task, you think you're actually paying attention to everything around you at the same time. But you're actually not." The brain is forced to switch among multiple cognitive tasks, as these tasks use the same part of the brain.[36]

The catch here is that this task-switching, despite how fast it occurs, is incredibly unproductive in reality—I mean like social networking unproductive. In fact, research indicates that up to *40 percent of productivity* could be lost due to task-switching. It actually takes more time to complete the tasks you're switching between and you make more errors than when you focus on doing one task at a time in order.[37]

A Stanford study confirmed this by showing that multitaskers are indeed worse performers, and struggle because they can't filter out irrelevant information, slowing down completion of the cognitive task at hand.[38] Additionally, studies have shown that it takes four times longer for the brain to recognize new things (further slowing down task completion), and that we have a much lower retention rate of what we learn while we are multitasking.[39]

The inefficiency of interrupting a task and starting another has long been known by factory managers, who seek to minimize the number of "changeovers" on the assembly lines (a changeover being when you stop running the line to start up production of a new or slightly different product). The task switching and startup time to get the line running at its previous high speed greatly dampens productivity.

The key is to accept the fundamental fact that the mind can do only one thing at a time.

And ditch the device when you're trying to be in the moment; it's often the primary co-conspirator in our multitasking offenses. Certainly, this is easier said than done, particularly because recent brain research indicates that our addiction to texts, Twitter, and Google has a physiological cause—the body's emission of dopamine, which I introduced you to earlier. Our brain gets pleasure when we seek and find new information, so it chemically encourages more such behavior.

To break this stimulation, experts say turn off the audio and visual cues built into your devices that alert you to the presence of more information. But mostly, just draw a line in the mental sandbox and commit to one thing at a time.[40]

2. *Catch the Drift.* I don't mean make sure you understand, although that's always good. I mean make it a point to notice when your attention is drifting. Excuse yourself and admit where you are mentally if you have to—faking it is frustrating and people will see through it.

Write yourself simple reminders to stay present like "Don't zone out, zone in," or "Be mindful, not mind full," or "Run your mind, don't let it run you." Anytime you catch yourself drifting, ask yourself, "What has my attention right now?"[41]

To further stay focused, commit to cease and desist with your inner monologue.

Or think of those you're interacting with as your customers. You'd never drift off on a customer for fear of losing an important sale.

You can also find an anchor for your thoughts, tethering your mind so it doesn't wander and so that you can better focus on the task at hand. For example, one psychotherapist suggests enabling refocusing by slowly breathing through your nose, which induces a relaxation response and helps settle the mind. This is why some martial arts instructors have their students train with a mouthful of water.[42]

Plain and simple, don't assume future moments are more important than the one you're in. It's important to give energy to trying to become; but sometimes it's just as important to simply be. It's about balance. *Become* starts with *be* for a reason.

The only thing that's real is the moment you're actually in—so live it.

And no, I didn't steal that off of a coffee mug in a gift shop.

3. *When frazzled, freeze.* It's so easy to zone out when you're tired, when you're running into your sixth back-to-back meeting on

something that requires attention. If you find yourself in this spot, don't let that next meeting get started without freezing for a moment.

Ask for a pause, go get a drink of water and clear your head or go check your lotto numbers for that matter. Assuming you didn't win, you're then ready to return to work—armed with a little mental stamina boost.

End the previous meeting a bit early to allow space for this if you're starting to feel burned-out. If you don't, once that next meeting starts, you'll quickly fall behind, and it's hard to catch up without alerting everyone to the fact that you haven't been paying attention.

You can also plan for these breathers by putting space on your calendar in between meetings. The space between your ears will be more engaged in the long run.

4. *Feel the meeting.* Don't just passively take in information during a meeting. Notice what's in front of you—the people, the passions, the emotions, the energy, the intention of the information being transmitted. Maybe not so much when you catch someone subtly picking their nose, though. Anyway, the point is to observe others for what they are (the good things) and for what they're trying to do, not for what you want them to be.

Find a memory to take from each meeting, even if it's a short-term one. Research shows that the habit of noticing new things and deeply engaging in the nuances of the present moment puts you emphatically in the here and now. It even reduces aggression by taking ego out of play because you're focusing on what's in front of you, not what it says about you.[43]

5. *Send signals of absorption.* When you're fully present and truly comprehending what others are saying, they'll know. But it doesn't hurt to put reminder physical mechanisms in place to help you share and show your full-on presence. Remember to maintain eye contact, nod at important points, stop to clarify,

take notes, and openly demonstrate that you're really listening. Such triggers send the right message and help you fully receive messages.

EARNING RESPECT

It's hard to have respect for and believe in yourself when you feel that others don't.

But in trying to change that, here's the problem.

There are endless iterations of what draws one person to respect another. An attribute you detest in someone will draw great admiration from someone else. It's a fool's game to chase a random set of behaviors in hopes of maximizing your respectability.

The good news is that you can greatly increase your odds of earning respect without losing your soul.

Here's how.

First, use this simple but powerful framework to help you prioritize and organize the actions you take to strengthen your "respected-quotient."

It's based on three critical questions:

1. What can you *give* to earn respect?
2. What should you *resist* to earn respect?
3. What should you *exude* to earn respect?

Give, Resist, Exude. That's your framework.

Now, we populate this framework with the characteristics and behaviors that most commonly draw universal respect. I've combed through reams of social science research to identify these themes for you.

Figure 6-2 shows what we get when we do that:

FIGURE 6-2

FRAMEWORK FOR EARNING RESPECT

GIVE	More than you get, your time and knowledge, praise/credit, the extra 10 percent always, your POV and stick by it, feedback, your word and keep it, respect
RESIST **X**	Credit, gossip/sharing secrets, over-apologizing, negativity, blaming
EXUDE	Professionalism, accountability, mastery, transparency/authenticity, confidence, care/empathy, collaboration, a "class-act" vibe (respect, integrity, humility, calm)

Finally, pick the things from this now populated framework that come naturally to you and amplify them. Also, pick a few things that you need to work on and that you're most passionate about improving upon—and improve them.

You don't need to master every item in the framework and try to be all things to everyone. Earning respect must come from an authentic place if you want to accomplish your mission and still feel whole.

If you've lost respect because of mistakes you've made in the past, (a) you might be O.J. Simpson and/or (b) all you can do is address those mistakes and work to regain respect over time. Psychology teaches us that people naturally want to like and respect other people. If you've put up barriers to that end, work hard to tear them down with consistent and thoughtful behavior in the areas above.

They'll come around.

When you're feeling self-confident, that you can persevere, that you're fully present, and that you've earned the respect you deserve, your self-belief soars. It is then that you're most ready to receive the overtures of inspiration all around you.

Like the Polynesians in this chapter's opening, keep rowing until you get there.

The paradise you'll discover is well worth the effort.

7

Disconnectedness

(REVERSED)

IMAGINE, IF YOU will, that you've been granted the strange but wonderful power to see the exchange of energy between life forces all around you, visible to no one else but you.

OK, granted, you're not being given the power of flying or X-ray vision, or the power to understand what all the buttons on your three TV remotes do, but work with me here.

So, you're sitting in the airport watching as two old friends trade broad smiles and waves upon spotting one another—one from the waiting area, the other approaching while eagerly pulling a rolling suitcase behind. Each of the two are bathed in a soft blue hue that only you can see—their personal, core energy—the energy we all start with, and would be limited to were we to live a life of solitude.

As they draw closer, hold eye contact, and make more animated gestures to one another, you notice orange tendrils of energy begin to emit forth from each of them, reaching out to the other in long, graceful, winding cords. Each of their individual blue hues is now becoming tinged with warmer orange tones. By the time they embrace each other in a "So glad to see you!" hug, their sheen is now completely bright orange.

Their energy has completed a transition, at least for the time being, not unlike the blue to orange transformation a flame makes shortly after its birth.

And you have just witnessed the power of human connection—its end product the transformation of pale blue to vivid orange—an upgraded emission of brightness and warmth.

Inspiration is drawn to brightness and warmth.

I believe that such energy exchanges really do happen in this world. And while we may not be able to see its physical manifestation, is it so implausible to believe that inspiration can?

When we become disconnected from those in our work life (whom we spend so much time with), we deny ourselves the exchange of the crackling orange tendrils of energy we draw from such connections. And so, we never fully ignite and burn our brightest; our personal energy can accomplish only so much, as formidable as it might be. We are thus destined to bathe only in our own pale blue light, with inspiration passing by like a ship in the much darker blue night.

This is what's at stake here.

The Anti-Muse of Disconnectedness longs to snuff out our orange flame.

The good news, though, is that to invite the energy additives in and keep the beacon for inspiration at its brightest, you don't need to be granted the power of strange vision.

You just need vision.

Vision, that is, to see yourself fully reconnected, with the right approach and plan in tow.

And here's the thing about being disconnected from anything, a coworker, a phone call, or a conga line—with intentionality you can always reconnect. It's a temporary break (like boy bands take before reuniting to rake in obscene amounts of money).

Just making the choice to reestablish connections with those who count can be inspiring, especially if it has been "a long time coming."

So, let's get those connections rewired and send a shimmering signal flare for inspiration to come calling.

THE CHAIN OF CAMARADERIE

If we were disconnected from our nuclear family, it would weigh on us tremendously, making it almost impossible to feel inspired each day. This isn't hard to understand given how sacred we hold the family unit (even after they've told us for the ninth time how to live our life).

Interestingly enough, research indicates that we're actually spending more time with coworkers than family; this is true of almost 80 percent of people who work thirty to fifty hours a week.[1] So, it's probably not surprising that research also indicates that we're increasingly viewing our coworkers as direct extensions of our family.[2]

By default, then, being disconnected from our coworkers is growing increasingly problematic for us.

And when we do truly connect with our work compatriots, research clearly indicates that it can indeed make us more passionate about and inspired by our work.[3] These stronger one-to-one connections add up to a greater whole as well. Studies show that top-rated places to work (with an inherently inspired workforce) share a sense of camaraderie as a key ingredient in their success formula.[4]

Furthermore, neuroscience research indicates that our brains are actually hard-wired to connect with others, so being disconnected from coworkers is not only an inspiration-killer, it's fighting Mother Nature herself.[5]

That might explain the astounding "add-on" effects of camaraderie in the workplace; nearly 40 percent of survey respondents named their coworkers as the top reason they love working for their company, 66 percent said those positive relationships increased their productivity, and 55 percent said they helped mitigate their on-the-job stress levels.[6] And 45 percent said that camaraderie with coworkers led to more Xerox-facilitated pictures of butts.

Another study showed that the factor most closely linked to physical and mental health at work is the support of coworkers—and not things you'd expect like the number of hours worked.[7]

The key, then, is the strength of the connection that you forge with your coworkers. Even if you wouldn't call yourself disconnected, there is always room to strengthen the bond—like in all those buddy-cop movies. To induce inspiration and beyond requires going beyond—from mere collaboration to camaraderie.

This is where a framework I call the "Chain of Camaraderie" comes into play (see Figure 7-1).

Picture a sturdy, thick length of chain, like the one in Figure 7-1. Now imagine that each link in the chain represents the ideal behaviors for facilitating a strong sense of camaraderie within a

FIGURE 7-1

THE CHAIN OF CAMARADERIE

group. You can instigate such behaviors, and in doing so, fully reconnect with and be inspired by your coworkers and your relationship with them.

To do so, it's helpful to consider three parts of the chain: the *center link*, to which each outer link connects; the *supporting links*, which constitute the substance of the chain itself; and the *weak links*, which can threaten the integrity of the chain. Let's examine each set of links.

The Center Link

Camaraderie and connection with thy fellow worker starts with three centerpiece elements: (1) shared purpose, (2) trust and truth, and (3) mutual respect.

It starts with a sense of common purpose and a "we're in it together" spirit. Studies show that soldiers form strong bonds during missions because they all believe in the purpose of the mission itself, and further unite through the need to rely on each other and to share the good and bad outcomes of the mission with their team.[8]

If your team has a purpose you can rally behind, do so. If not, take the initiative to articulate one in concert with your teammates. Additionally, ensure that the goals that accompany the purpose are specific and crystal clear. The combination of a compelling purpose and clear goals is a galvanizing force to be reckoned with.

I intentionally pair trust and truth because they're so intertwined. Having a foundation of trust in place encourages the truth being spoken, and continually speaking the truth further strengthens trust. Both are absolutely essential to creating and maintaining a sense of camaraderie.

Lean forward and show your trust in others, be trustworthy yourself, and model speaking and accepting the truth, always. Members of Congress can skip this section altogether, of course.

Finally, camaraderie simply can't exist without mutual respect. Don't make the mistake of assuming this is a commonsense/throwaway point. Eye-opening research indicates that employees rank "respectful treatment of all employees at all levels" as the number one most important factor for job satisfaction. Sadly, however, this was also the area of greatest disparity between what employees valued most and their level of satisfaction.[9] (Hopefully you found help on this front in the section on earning respect in Chapter 6.)

Believe me, your coworkers won't feel like you're overdoing it if you go beyond merely getting to know them to unearthing more reasons to genuinely respect them—and then interacting with them as such each and every day.

It's important to point out at this juncture that strong connections with your coworkers don't require you to be lifetime besties (although, of course, that's always nice). University of Michigan professor Jane Dutton has found that strong connections in the workplace don't require "a deep or intimate relationship." Just one interaction underscored with mutual engagement and marked by the core factors of trust and respect can generate enough energy from both parties to transform transaction-based interactions into a relationship.[10]

Supporting Links

There are many supporting links in the Chain of Camaraderie; the more links forged the greater your chances of inviting inspiration back into your workdays. Here are nine such powerful links—many leverage the power of reciprocity—engage in this behavior and you'll get it right back.

Nine Ways to Cultivate Camaraderie

1. *Create* purposeful *bonding experiences.* The first instinct for many seeking to build a sense of camaraderie is to amp up the amount of socializing.

Now, there's nothing wrong with grabbing a cocktail with your cohorts. However, relying solely on socializing to build bonds may not be as effective as you think. Research shows that people "don't mix much at mixers," and they mostly bond with similar colleagues at company functions.[11] I suspect the exception is the infamous holiday office party where two drinks in people are "bonding" in the supply closet.

Anyway, the idea is to be intentional and design a breadth of experiences with a specific purpose in mind to aid in the bonding process. Four types of specific experiences tend to be most effective in building camaraderie:

a. Shared experiences of substance—including celebration of team successes and failures, opportunities to have fun and learn together as a team, and opportunities to work together on a tough problem. Experiencing the same things with a community of others, whether good or bad, instinctively pulls people closer together. Unless it's an office outing to see *The Book of Mormon.*

Anyway, failure to get collectively involved in experiences of substance can have consequences beyond even the failure to find inspiration. A study showed that 74 percent of surveyed employees who hadn't celebrated accomplishments with their coworkers said they were more likely to leave their jobs.[12]

b. Shared identity experiences—opportunities to work as a team to accomplish a specific mission that could only be achieved by that team. Such opportunities strengthen the collective team identity to which individual members have assimilated themselves and enhance the desire to belong.

Relatedly, creating artifacts to further strengthen one's association with a team are important. Such artifacts include distinct naming nomenclature ("Team Apollo," "The Everest Team," etc.) and symbols of membership for such teams (like logos, badges, or slogans) that further enhance the sense of belonging.

Flaming skull tattoos for everyone can help as well.

c. Shared crucible moments—including opportunities to make a critical decision, react to a crisis, or set a compelling vision—all as a unified team. This is about being alert as an inspiration instigator and on the lookout for key moments that require, and reward, cohesion.

d. Appreciation-enhancing experiences—namely rituals that shine the spotlight on an individual and that person's accomplishments and/or enable more to be learned about him or her. Such experiences bolster respect, admiration, and the desire for a deeper connection as new things are learned about the person. Appreciation-enhancing experiences also elevate the level of commitment, as no one wants to let down a teammate recognized as talented and accomplished (especially if that teammate has access to the company box at the football stadium).

2. *Spread positive gossip.* Get caught talking about your coworkers, in an upbeat way. The cold truth is that the Anti-Muse of Disconnectedness is far too masterful at enlisting an army of naysayers, critics, and backstabbers. Swim upstream. When the wisps of goodwill organically make their way back to the protagonist, it has a powerful, connective impact; we're instinctively drawn to our supporters. And inspiration will take note of the effort.

3. *Play your position; be in position to play.* This isn't just the old platitude of work hard/play hard. This is first about knowing *what* to work hard at. This means knowing what your role in the assembly line is and being prepared and feeling accountable to deliver it with excellence, then reliably doing so. This is opposed to the misguided effort of trying to involve yourself in everything and know everything in an attempt to be the hero for the team. The reality is that people will be drawn to your competence but repelled by your omnipotence.

After giving your unique responsibilities everything you've got, it's about that not being all that you give. Save some mental energy and capacity to unwind and enjoy with the very coworkers alongside whom you've been working so hard. While I indicated earlier that people tend not to "mix at mixers," it's different for a group that has been working hard together. Again, social bonding can be an effective contributor to camaraderie, as long as it's part of a balanced portfolio of efforts.

4. *Give them 10 percent more.* We all know how it feels when you see a waiter, sales clerk, or flight attendant give that extra effort. You feel important and cared for and have an urge to reward their dedication in some form. Maybe by re-gifting your Starbucks gift card even though you've already bought two lattes with it. Hey, it's the thought that counts, you reason. Anyway, you get the instant sense that you can count on such people.

It's no different with our coworkers. Making a conscious effort to put 10 percent more into what you're helping them with, or into your own work, will be noticed by a factor of ten. The extra respect and appreciation granted will go a long way toward accelerating a sense of camaraderie.

5. *Increase your "click quotient."* Research shows that some of us have a greater natural ability to "click" with others, that is, to quickly find ways to connect with others and rapidly establish rapport. Such people are easy to chat with at a cocktail party. I've always imagined Tom Hanks and Ellen DeGeneres to be like this. I'm guessing they feel the same about me.

University of Minnesota psychologist Mark Snyder calls such people "high self-monitors." He discovered that high self-monitors are social chameleons. Snyder says, "Without even realizing it, they adapt their personalities, behavior, and attitudes to fit the people around them. They pick up subtle social cues and tailor their responses to the situation."

Such an approach not only aids in fast-forwarding toward camaraderie, but it also highly correlates with success. Studies from other universities showed that high self-monitors had established a strong network of supporters and comrades at work in just eighteen months (which clearly helped their career progression, a source of inspiration in and of itself) while low self-monitors took an astonishing thirteen years to do so.[13]

Now, by no means am I suggesting that you alter the core essence of who you are with each social encounter. And by no means am I suggesting that if you don't have a natural affinity for this, you're doomed.

Rather, increasing your click quotient is about being authentic *and* adaptable. For example, meeting up with someone who is high energy? Even if this is not your defining trait, adapt to the situation and play your energy up as much as you can. Everything and everyone you connect with doesn't have to be a perfect match—it's not how the real world works.

It's about selecting from your own authentic portfolio of characteristics and dialing them up and down as needed, and even tacking on socially savvy behaviors from time to time (even if they aren't your preferred ones). Doing so will raise your "click quotient" and help give you a starting point from which you can build a deeper connection.

You can also increase this quotient by being vulnerable. When we're vulnerable and open up, it immediately induces a sense of trust and makes us more relatable. Research from social psychologist Arthur Aron proved this point in a study that paired strangers up, placed them in one of two groups, and then gave each group a set of different questions to discuss. One group chatted over trivial questions, like "What did you do over the holiday?" while the other discussed deeper, more revealing topics, like "What are your most treasured memories?"

The pairs in the latter group formed "incredibly quick, deep connections." Two of these test subjects even got married.[14] (I'm sure the researcher didn't realize he was running Test-Lab Tinder.)

The net of this is that if you take a chance, are vulnerable, and open up, you can open up connections—that endure.

6. *Invite their gifts in.* Nothing enhances a sense of belongingness and feeling valued more than being asked to share the things that make you so valuable in the first place. When people appreciate the unique you, it creates a bond. You can help facilitate this by creating an environment where others feel comfortable, appreciated, and warmly invited to share their unique talents. They'll return the favor.

7. *Practice "cut the cord" communication.* The firefighting profession is one that demands camaraderie among its practitioners. After all, it's quite possible on any given day that one firefighter will have to save the life of another. Stephen Marsar is a veteran and captain in the vaunted Fire Department City of New York (FDNY), and a firehouse chief who understands this. Marsar teaches and preaches the importance of developing a deep sense of camaraderie among firefighters.

And his manner for achieving this may surprise you.

Marsar borrows a page from your parents. Remember how much they wanted the family to gather around the dinner table and just talk to each other while sharing a meal? Marsar insists on this during shared meals in the firehouse (called a fire*house* for a reason, according to Marsar). It's a method that's been proven in research to be incredibly effective. To enable this, he has instituted a "cut the cord" communication policy—no devices, nothing with a cord, (no iPad, iPhone, or i-anything) are allowed at the dinner table. Just i-present. This forces the firefighters to really communicate with each other. Maybe even *t-a-l-k* to one another.[15]

Carry this philosophy metaphorically (and even literally) into your work relationships. Put down the device, or turn off the one in your head, and just . . . listen. Comprehend. Ask questions. Respond. The bottom line is to be all-in when communicating so you're not left out of camaraderie.

8. *Openly and subtly have their backs.* Visibly backing one another up is one of the best ways to move camaraderie forward. Help your compatriots solve a circumstance, be on the lookout for ways to help and support them, put the effort in to share information they could benefit from, accept their imperfections, and be their fiercest advocates.

Just as powerful, you can look for those quiet moments, when no one else is looking, where you can help create a positive impression of them or help move something forward that's important to them, like a project or even their career. If your subtle efforts ever do get back to the recipient, it has a multiplicative bonding impact.

Net: When you have someone's back and they have yours, it builds bonds and a bridge—to inspiration.

9. *Exude the bellwether behaviors of camaraderie.* There are four such behaviors in two closely related sets: Care and Compassion, and Energy and Inquiry. Care enough about your cohorts to be interested in them. Care what they think, notice and remember things about them, root for them and enjoy their successes, help them grow with thoughtful feedback, and just do something nice for them from time to time. Be compassionate enough to be inclusive to all and to make it OK for any of them to be vulnerable and make mistakes, while showing vulnerability yourself.

Be all-in and exude positive, authentic energy that will draw others to you. Eight-year-old children instinctively have a sense for this—they know who to invite to their birthday parties and who not to, based on the type of energy the other eight-year-olds bring. So, believe me, your coworkers have an opinion on if they want you around or not. Positive, authentic energy helps put you on the invite list (as does owning a boat).

And be inquisitive—about them, about how you can contribute more value to the team, about problems the team is facing, and about how to make things better for everyone in general.

Weak Links

Camaraderie can afford no weak links in the chain. There are three especially common such links that can threaten the strength and integrity of the chain: (a) unhealthy debate, (b) difficult co-workers, and (c) a difficult boss.

Unhealthy Debate

Psychology researcher Dr. John Gottman can predict whether or not a married couple will be together five years later with startling 90 percent accuracy. How does he do it?

He watches them argue.

The ability to engage in healthy, productive debate, without spiraling down into harmful conflict and rifts, turns out to be essential for ensuring long-term success, for maintaining a sense of camaraderie, and for helping ideas blossom.

A team of Berkeley researchers discovered that teams that debated their ideas had 25 percent more ideas altogether. Lead researcher Charlan Nemeth said, "Our findings show that debate and criticism do not inhibit ideas but, rather, stimulate them relative to every other condition."[16] And ideas inspire.

Researchers and marriage mavens aren't the only ones who have figured out the power of a debate-encouraging process—some pretty smart companies have too.

Like Pixar.

The animation powerhouse has imbued daily debate as part of its DNA. They gather as a team and criticize the previous day's work—everybody gets run through the gamut, and no detail is too small to be debated. The process is absolutely vital to the consistent production of such high-quality work.[17]

The lesson here is that you have to fundamentally believe that conflict is beneficial and even essential for producing ongoing greatness and closeness, and thus in turn inviting inspiration in.

You have to believe that conflict requires conviction, and that conviction must be grounded in something worth at least listening to. You have to know that decisions by default versus debate are decisions undone. And you should know that encouraging healthy debate is like being inside a plastic bag—when people poke holes, you can ultimately breathe easier (i.e., be confident in a decision well-vetted).

The art of enabling healthy tension should get your attention, because the payoff is worth it. But encouraging debate isn't always easy—human nature gets in the way.

And by that I mean we can be wusses.

Debate can be uncomfortable and is often viewed as the sign of a bad meeting—and bad meetings are often feared more than bad results. Here are nine ways to help make the necessary process of debate more amenable to all.

Nine Ways to Cultivate Healthy Debate

1. *Separate the person from the point.* Ever experience an escalating debate that you sense is getting fueled by underlying relationship issues? The conflict arises over the relationship, not the idea at hand; points made start to come with an edge to them and soon start feeling like thinly veiled personal attacks. The truth is that it's all too easy to let tension in a relationship push healthy debate into heal thy-self debate. Whether you feel the sting of such debate directly or are witness to it, such discourse needs to be squashed and redirected back to debate squarely focused on the merits of an idea. And until the relationship is repaired, debate will rarely be healthy. Period.

2. *Encourage animated, not heated, debate.* The distinction made here to the previous point is that debates can unproductively escalate even among those without relationship issues. The cofounder and CTO of Hubspot, Dharmesh Shah, draws a distinction between heated and animated debates. While heated

is argumentative and discouraged, Shah says that "Animated is when you get passionate because you care about [the] issue"; which is definitely welcomed.[18]

To keep ideas on the front burner but with the heat dialed down, remind participants of common goals. This can go a long way toward diffusing the emotion involved.

3. *Enroll early.* It's harder for people to objectively listen to input when they're too far down the road on something. Tempers rise because so much work has been done already and debate at that point is less welcome because it could mean work unwound. Make a list of who gets to debate an idea and bring them in early in the process. The much-needed discussion will be much more productive.

4. *Think commitment, not compliance.* The goal of any decision made is to have fierce commitment to it, not mere compliance (notwithstanding your child's bedtime, to which you'll desperately take mere compliance in lieu of commitment—to a mental institution).

The point is when you eagerly make efforts to hear every voice at the table (dissenting or not), people will feel heard. And you know the adage about people needing to weigh in before they can buy in. Giving every opportunity for healthy debate before deciding helps you garner deep commitment to the outcome, not just surface-level compliance.

5. *Ask that opinions be grounded, not unfounded.* Debates can turn unproductive when unchecked opinion becomes the norm. Opinions, while important (of course), must be balanced with facts and supporting data. Otherwise people start tuning out or discussion heads in an unhelpful direction.

6. *Be mindful of an open mind.* To help you keep an open mind, absolutely essential to healthy debate, remember General George

S. Patton, who said "If everyone is thinking alike, then somebody isn't thinking."[19] He may have also started that whole "Keep Calm" thing by saying "Keep Calm and Open Fire," but I can't prove that.

Anyway, if there is a continual lack of dissent around you, it should send signal flares that it's time for you to examine your own behaviors. You should let counterpoints raise interest, not hackles, and role model the right behavior at such junctures.

To further help you keep an open mind, make a habit of recalling when you've been wrong and reminding yourself that conflict ultimately brings resolution faster (and a smarter resolution at that).

7. *Kill debate killers.* There's nothing worse than a good, productive debate brought to a screeching halt.

This happens when debaters drone on or frequently interrupt. Poorly framed discussions, hidden agendas, leading questions, and witch-hunting (blame seeking) versus fact finding all contribute to debate-gone-dead as well.

A culture of meetings after the meeting also cripple good debate, as attendees figure they don't have to speak their mind because they can speak it afterwards in a post-mortem meeting. Skirted debates turn into sour grapes, and avoidance of debate altogether can become habit.

Be on the lookout to squash these destructive behaviors.

8. *Commend, not condemn, the opposing point of view.* Those who stand up and speak their mind should stand out and be on your mind. Remember their brave behavior and reward it. Nothing encourages more of the behavior you want like rewarding the behavior you want.

9. *Plus it up.* Pixar practices this. Criticism must always contain a new idea or a suggestion for strengthening the original idea—it must contain a "plus." This ensures a positive tone, maintains

respect, and keeps ideas growing and changing for the better.[20] The desire for debate thus escalates.

Difficult Coworkers

This weak-link counter to camaraderie (and resultant inspiration) is all too common. We all could name a coworker we find more annoying than a selfie-stick.

In fact, research indicates that 85 percent of us have to deal with workplace conflict to some degree, with personality clashes and warring egos being the culprit half the time.[21] Now, as I stated earlier, by no means should you assume that you have to be friends with everyone, although being *friendly* to everyone is a good policy. The solution has many variables, all of which flow from the need to *STEP BACK*:

Stop wishing they were different:[22] It's important to give all co-workers, difficult or not, room to be themselves and to stop the futility of wishing otherwise. Much of improving relationships with difficult coworkers is about trying to change the *interchange,* not trying to change *them.* And ask yourself if you're really just substituting the word *difficult* for *different.*[23] Embrace their differences, avoid labeling them, and admit that you have the opportunity to learn from them. Be mindful to keep the focus on the predicament, not the personality.

Take the initiative: No good can come from waiting to address the situation of a difficult coworker. You have to take responsibility for the relationship and not let things fester. And make no mistake, merely "troubling" can quickly turn to "toxic." Decide what your desired outcome is and what behaviors to address or ignore and get to work on opening the lines of communication in an upfront and respectful way. When you talk *to,* and not *about* the coworker, you've started down the high road, and will be on the road to re-covering a more complete sense of camaraderie.[24]

Ego may be the culprit, so set it aside: As stated earlier, research indicates that warring egos are a big cause of workplace con-flict, the primary cause in fact.[25] Second is whoever refuses to clean out the damn microwave after their Spaghetti-O's boil over. Anyway, be self-aware if your ego is creeping in as a cause of conflict and on alert if the coworker's ego is in play. Adjust your approach to avoid further attacking their ego while keeping your own in check.

Proceed with curiosity, not contempt: Think of difficult cowork-ers as offering a fascinating study in human behavior. Take an interest in getting to the why's behind their behavior by getting to know them better, as difficult as it may be. As-sume that there's an underlying reason for the way they interact with you and seek to understand. Such under-standing will always serve you well and is more productive than letting your ire dictate your approach.

Begin with you: Analyze *your* reactions to difficult encounters first and foremost. Are you overreacting and fueling the fire? Are you truly being your best self in dealing with the situa-tion and practicing enough self-control? Are you exuding calm and as much positivity and objectivity as possible?

Assumptions on intention must stop: Misinterpreted inten-tions are another primary cause of unhealthy workplace conflict. Don't assume the intentions of an offending co-worker; instead seek to understand their point of view (in-cluding carefully getting perspective from others). Difficult people rarely see themselves that way. There are almost always perfectly legitimate reasons for their behavior, such as differing reward systems, insecurities, lack of training, or the fact that they were raised as Kentucky basketball fans.

Create small bridges: At work, and in life, little olive branches and acts of kindness, empathy, validation, and forgiving can go a long way toward making connections and helping a relationship to a better place. Make the effort to build little bridges of connectivity with the individual. Drop the defensiveness and default to acknowledgment, not argument. Find things you have in common and build on them. Try to overlook that they're the kind of person who, on an elevator, fake searches for the "open" button as someone is dashing to get on.

You get the idea.

Even if you feel affronted, recognize that they very likely feel the same way. Andy Selig, an organizational psychologist and mediator of workplace tensions, says: "Most of the time, all the protagonists involved feel like victims."[26] Recognize this and be willing to "be the bigger person."

Know that you choose how much power you'll give them over you.[27] Much of this list has been about what you can do to alter the weakening effect a difficult coworker can have on camaraderie. It's quite possible that you will run into truly toxic behaviors or individuals who defy "repair."

In such cases, to keep a sense of camaraderie intact, you have to define how much you'll let such individuals impact you and your outlook. You have to put such people into perspective within the context of your pursuit of camaraderie as a beacon for inspiration. Ultimately you may simply have to mentally manage down the negative impact you'll let them have on you.

A Difficult Boss

Here's a shocker. Your manager has a disproportionate impact on the amount of inspiration you're able to feel at work. Kidding aside, far too many employees report that their boss not only doesn't evoke any sense of inspiration, he or she eviscerates it. This relationship is so important that I will address it separately in Chapter 10, "Lack of Evocation (Rediscovered)," so that you can learn how to actually convert that critical relationship into one that regularly evokes a sense of inspiration.

The Anti-Muse of Disconnectedness has kept us separated from inspiration for long enough. Inspiration is drawn to the warm energy we exchange with our work mates in the midst of a great relationship.

Having made the connection now, it's time to start wiring and firing these connections.

8

Dearth of Creating
(RECONSTITUTED)

I INTERVIEWED OR surveyed thousands of uninspired employees along with undertaking hefty academic research for this book. No admission came with more resignation and wistfulness from respondents than this one, summed up in this exchange:

"What has caused you to lose your inspiration?"

A long pause followed by, "I somehow stopped creating."

The employee then goes on to eloquently explain:

When I'm creating I feel alive and free. My little creations are my unique contributions to the world that shout "I'm here and I have an imprint!" The form of creativity doesn't matter—an idea of mine brought to market, a concept I thought of shared in a written recommendation, or a sketch that got incorporated into a design. Anything imaginative that wouldn't have happened were it not for me inspires me to do it again and makes my spirit soar. I told a

friend recently that I've somehow sunk into constant transaction mode, with no room for transcendent mode. This
place has stifled my creativity. It has clipped my wings.

The amazing thing about this professed absence of creating
was how it most often surfaced. It wasn't always the first thing
respondents said. (The first thing was usually "Am I getting paid
for this?") Most came to the realization, right in front of me, that
a sense of creativity and innovation was sorely missing from their
lives. It took stopping to think about how their days were spent,
how transactional it had all become, which in turn reminded
them how much they enjoyed what they *weren't* getting to—
unique, creative contributions.

I unearthed so many "Holy crap, I stopped creating!" moments
that I stopped counting.

It occurred to me that there may be a more deep-seated reason
for the explosion in popularity of coloring books—*for adults.*

An Anti-Muse of stealth and distraction, this one.

I think it's safe to say that reigniting this part of us is absolutely
vital.

In fact, it produces a powerful virtuous cycle; when we create
we become inspired, and when we're inspired, we create.

Psychologists Todd Thrash and Andrew Elliot have actually
drawn a mathematical correlation between creativity and inspiration. One unlikely group of research subjects was especially
effective in confirming the correlation—U.S. patent holders.
Thrash and Elliot indicated that patent holders, motivated by
novel ideas and moved to translate their ideas into reality, were
"found to be inspired more frequently and more intensely"
than a random sample of university alumni. In fact, the frequency of their inspiration was directly related to the number
of patents held.[1]

The very act of creating further inspired the patent holders—
as it does us.

So your question at this point is likely either (a) "I get the cor-relation between creativity and inspiration, but can I actually re-kindle my creativity?" or (b) "Am I getting paid for this?"

Let's focus on the first question, which requires us to first an-swer a different question. Can creativity be learned?

A team of researchers led by innovation guru Clayton Chris-tensen (author of *The Innovator's Dilemma*) say you absolutely can learn to be more creative. Their research indicates that the most innovative CEOs weren't just naturally born that way—they spent 50 percent more time on creativity-building skills than other CEOs did.[2]

And if creativity can be learned in the first place, it can cer-tainly be reconstituted.

To help you do that requires more than a lot of research, em-ployee interviews, and personal experience. As creativity doesn't happen in a vacuum, neither does stimulation for learning how to trigger it in the first place.

Accordingly, I assembled a Creative Board of Directors to ad-vise me. I sought out experts to help ensure that I had the best possible approach to helping people rekindle their sense of cre-ativity. The standard I held as I selected my board was that each expert's occupation had to come with an inherent *vested interest* in stimulating creativity. Some stakes in the game.

And so I enrolled a group with such credentials as chief inno-vation officer, chief brand officer, Hollywood producer, Holly-wood director, head chef of a renowned five-star restaurant, advertising agency creative directors, president of an innovation think tank, director of a Fortune 50 Innovation Lab, VPs of mar-keting, artists, musicians, authors who write about unlocking cre-ativity, speakers who speak about unlocking creativity, and podcasters who podcast about unlocking creativity.

Combining research, interviews, experience, and insight from my Creative Board of Directors, what follows is a portfolio of op-tions for rekindling one's creativity at work (and in life).

THE STEM METHOD

Creativity can be reignited (and inspiration invited back in) by leveraging the right *Stimulus*, by employing the right *Techniques*, by altering your *Environment*, and by adopting the right *Mindset—STEM.*

This method doesn't require that you take on everything that follows. Rather, it's meant to serve as a portfolio of proven options from which you can pick the ones that most speak to you.

Stimulus

- *No input/No output*—Hollywood director, writer, producer, and inspiration for the CBS show *The Crazy Ones,* John Montgomery, told me about the importance of being open to new experiences:

  > Record companies would ask Joe Strummer of the Clash, "Where's your next album?" He'd respond, "No input, no output." Sitting around a studio would not lead to a new album. Creativity is contingent upon experiencing life. In Hollywood, too many writers spend preposterous hours in the writers' room, searching internally for inspiration, when creativity can be found in the world around them. Their approach is hard-wired for sameness.

  > Through my own experiences working with creatives at advertising agencies, I can tell you that their best creative inspiration came when they "weren't working"—when they went on long lunches to catch a Broadway show, went to see a late-night stand-up act, etc.

  > While finding time to take these experiential breaks can be tough, it's a must for opening up our minds. As Todd Henry, creativity expert and author of *The Accidental Creative,* put it, "We tend to work in a massive echo-chamber."

Dan Cohen, SVP and creative director at the Publicis Groupe advertising agency, would agree with all of this and then take it a step further. Cohen's take on getting input from the outside world is a process of what he calls "getting cross-trained."

Cohen told me that to enhance the frequency and quality of his creativity, he strives to stay well-rounded. So he "cross-trains" by going beyond his day job to engage in hobbies, extra projects, getting behind a cause, doing something artistic—all in the pursuit of becoming more well-rounded. This approach, by the way, also helps him to be more efficiently creative. Says Cohen, "The busier you are, the more productive you are, and the more creative you are as you're forced to be crafty to get everything done."

- *Ask for the worst assignment*—Cohen also likes to seek out the assignments that others don't want. It's a good challenge, he says, but more important, there's less pressure, the bar is lower, and he has more breathing room to be creative. "You can go from worst to first with a crazy drunk-a$# idea," as he told me.
- *Find inherently interesting challenges*—When I first started writing my column for *Inc.*, the first dozen articles I wrote were all based on very specific assignments *Inc.* editors gave me (I mean other than the general assignment of "Don't suck."). I was asked to write about a universal problem for entrepreneurs and give advice on how to solve it, write about a relevant big name in the news and lessons to be gleaned from their story, write about a workplace issue that requires immediacy in resolution, and so on. Each challenge was specific and stimulating, and in turn stimulated my creativity.

So go on the hunt for specific challenges to solve that interest you. Your inherent desire to solve those challenges will get your creative juices flowing.

- *Find a pressing problem/opportunity or an intensely desired goal*—
Related to the above point, success guru Brian Tracy says
finding an urgent problem/opportunity or a hugely desired goal are two methods sure to stimulate creativity, and
I couldn't agree more. The key is to sharpen the pressing
problem or opportunity so it's clearly understood, which
in turn focuses your energy and maximizes chances for
successfully coming up with a creative solution.

  Heidi Sandreuter, VP of women's marketing for Under
Armour at the time the company was awarded "Marketer
of the Year" by *Advertising Age,* agrees too. As Sandreuter
told me, "The absolute best way to unlock creativity is to
give the freedom of a tight brief." In other words, have the
problem or opportunity so clearly defined that it gives the
freedom of laser-like focus to direct energy and sharpen
output. Armed with such a clear definition, you can address the problem with what Brian Tracy calls "confident
expectancy."[3]

  Similarly, get crystal clear on the desired goal to pursue.
And the higher the bar set by that goal, by the way, the
better for stimulating creativity.

- *Create a watershed moment*—Bruce Hall, president of Eureka!
Inventing, a company that helps enable innovation, says he
sees one thing in particular far too often across the myriad
of companies he works with (besides overzealous
badge-checkers).

  He encounters employees who reward themselves with
maintenance—sticking to the tried and true, not taking
any risks, not rocking the boat.

  One of the most important things Hall and his company
do to shake up the corporate cocoon and fire up creativity
is to push for creation of a watershed moment, a turning
point. It's a special kind of high bar because it comes with
emotional resonance and personal meaning. Says Hall,

I like to challenge my clients to stop the insanity of business as usual. I challenge them to craft a moment in history when everything changed for the better. Their goal should be to say "I was there when...." I tell them if they want to hide in the organization, then they have to live with the consequences of that. Instead, they can stand up and say "I'm going to have an impact." When I do this, I give them permission to be creative once again, forgetting all the things holding them back from doing so. And then . . . magic happens.

- *Uncover real insight from those who buy what you sell*—There's something exhilarating about uncovering an insight that isn't just true, it's *sooo* true. Researchers for Iams pet food found out their buyers tended to also buy Febreze—to help neutralize pet odors. OK. That's an insight. That's true. But they also discovered that the heaviest buyers of their product actually bought Christmas gifts for their pets, and wrapped them up before gifting them to their furred friends.

  That's an insight that's *sooo* true.

  And it inspires its own set of creative marketing activities accordingly. If you're a marketer, you almost *have* to do something armed with that knowledge.

  Now, of course, uncovering rich insight isn't easy. It requires a commitment to spend time with buyers to develop a deep understanding of them. But the payoff to unearthing deep insight is unlocking creativity.

- *Take inspiration from those who use what you sell*—Those who buy what you sell may not be the same as those who use what you sell. Even if they are the same person, studying usage can be enlightening. In Chapter 3, "Settling and Boredom (Rejected)," I highlighted how studying the end user could inspire risk-taking. Similarly, it can spark creativity. More than one VP of marketing told me that when things get stale creatively, they reconnect their team with the end user of their products. Better understanding the users' wants, needs, hopes, and aspirations and watching them use the products/services you provide can remind you of why you provide them in the first place. It rekindles interest in better serving that consumer and makes you more invested in applying creativity to do so.

One VP in the footwear industry told me that his company's biggest project in a decade came from having a small group of scientists and marketers watch the end user use their products in a New Jersey YMCA. The product innovation is expected to launch a sub-category for the company with conservative estimates north of a quarter-billion dollars in sales.

Not bad for soaking up the details of someone sweating in your product.

Technique

- *Iterate on the right things*—Many industry experts consider Taco Bell to be the most innovative restaurant chain in the business. It pumps out new product hit after new product hit. As of this writing, Taco Bell had churned out (in a relatively short window) hits like Crunchwraps, Doritos Locos Tacos, Quesalupas, Chalupas, a Starburst and Airheads line of drinks (based on the iconic candies), and many more. All meet Taco Bell's goal of offering a great food experience. I know, because I've tried them all. In the name of research, of course. And I may or may not have tried to write it all off as a business expense.

  Anyway, innovations so creative in nature crafted at such a rapid pace don't just magically happen. Liz Matthews, chief food innovation officer at Taco Bell, told me one of the secrets to their success lies in making creativity a team sport:

> Every Friday our team is together at the grocery store or watching people eat lunch, and we just share ideas. We iterate on those ideas all week, milling on them 24/7. We get together with our Creationeers (six chefs) and we ideate and iterate based on a problem to solve or an insight. We dream of what could be, take influences from other places, and connect dots to what we think our consumer might love. We don't spend months perfecting any one idea, we put it in front of our executive team very early in the process with no bureaucracy, no dog and pony. It really is a process of constant, rapid iteration and building off one another all the way up through the executive team. None of our mega-hits have come from an unfiltered idea from any one person—each idea that makes it to market represents a collective effort of energetic iteration.

I got a chance to witness this collective effort firsthand when the Taco Bell team invited me into their test kitchen. I participated in a spirited, multifunctional feedback session for a new creation the chefs were tasked with cooking up.

Matthews continued:

> By the way, the saying that no idea is a bad idea is wrong—there are plenty of bad ideas. The key is to identify them as such early on, kill them, and iterate on the ideas with the most potential. But along the way, you also have to believe that good ideas can come from anywhere. Lots of large organizations say this, but they don't believe it. We really do.

- *Try the fifth take*—Hollywood producer Mark Teitelbaum (along with his directing partner John Montgomery, previously mentioned), had the privilege of working with comedy legend Robin Williams before his tragic death. The trio were the driving forces behind *The Crazy Ones*, a David E. Kelly–backed CBS half-hour comedy and one of Williams's very last projects. Teitelbaum shared with me what he learned about unleashing creativity by watching Williams perform in the show's pilot episode, one of the greatest pilots ever made in Teitelbaum's estimation. As Teitelbaum tells it:

  > We were working a key scene in the episode, where Robin was sharing a tender moment with his daughter (played by Sarah Michelle Geller). We did four takes and were about to move on. Suddenly, Robin said, "Wait, can we do this just one more time?" We obliged, of course; this is Robin Williams we're talking about. Robin proceeded to go off script, improvising delivery of a heartfelt story in the voice of an Indian gentleman. The performance was unbelievably layered, textured, and nuanced. All we could do was sit in stunned admiration. Robin's improv became the best part of a pilot that was the best pilot I'd ever seen. I learned in that moment the power of going off-script, giving it that fifth take, and giving creative people runway to be creative.

  Our best creativity can often come from that last effort, the one where you let your hair down and improvise on the fly. So ask for that one more take, and take back a sense of creativity and inspiration.

- *Look for springboards*—Creativity isn't just forcefully sparked by trying to rebuild Rome on a tight deadline. It can take place in much smaller ways. Go on the hunt for relatively small things that you can make just a little bit better. Come up with one way you can make that weekly meeting just a bit more fun and efficient (besides canceling it). Think of ways to make the product's website a little more engaging or how to make the production line run a little faster. Challenge the status quo of everything around you, seeing the possibilities and looking beyond constraints. Before you know it, you'll be emboldened to move on to bigger, tougher problems in need of some serious creative thinking.

• *Borrow brilliance*—In his book *Steal Like an Artist,* author Austin Kleon says, "Nothing is original, so embrace influence, collect ideas, and remix and re-imagine to discover your own path."[4]

If it's true that nothing comes from nowhere, then just get on with the process of being influenced to jump-start your creativity. Don't set an impossibly high bar of profound originality. As Kleon goes on to say, "If we're free from the burden of trying to be completely original, we can stop trying to make something out of nothing, and we can embrace influence instead of running away from it."[5]

So borrow and be influenced. It's a loan that will pay interest—interest in your work again.

• *Open up the senses*—Creativity blossoms when we open our senses and look past what's in front of us. Famed Disney "Imagineers" use an interesting technique to practice this. They look at a painting, then answer these questions:

1. What does it smell like in this picture?
2. What do you see to the left of the picture? To the right?
3. What's the air temperature in this picture?

The exercise helps train the brain to think creatively by "looking past the edges" and by using all of one's senses.[6] You can do the same.

Imagine you're trying to figure out how to make your brand of cereal more noticeable on the shelf. You can start by looking at the box itself, the shelf, and the surrounding shelf signage for opportunities. These are the usual suspects.

But what would that box of cereal say to a child if it could? (voilà—ideas for talking shelf devices surface). What would that box smell like if you walked by it? (boom—on-shelf scent machines come to mind). What should the box feel like to a sight-impaired person? (shazam, ideas for textured packaging arise).

You get the point.

Use all your senses. Look past the edges. Push the limits by not stopping at what's expected or obvious. Creative Director Cohen, whom you met earlier, subscribes to this theory when developing advertising ideas for his clients. Says Cohen, "I do exactly what's asked first. Then I stretch it. I go beyond the edges. I push myself trying to find unobvious solutions that aren't creative just for the sake of being creative, but that solve a problem in an interesting, new way."

- *Use as much or as little process as you need*—Full confession here. Neither my Creative Board of Directors, the research, nor my experience pinpointed one set way to use process for unlocking creativity.

  Taco Bell's Matthews told me, "The second you start to put structure on innovation is when you lose innovation. The second someone says you have to come up with an idea, you flail. If you put pressure on people to come up with ideas, they're made-up ideas, not rooted in the consumer." This philosophy seems to be working at Taco Bell—they're pumping out ideas faster than a pissed-off mom can text.

  On the other hand, Eureka! Inventing has seen great success at creating a specific process for engineering innovation, even teaching it as a minor degree program at twenty universities. The process, influenced by W. Edwards Deming and his Six Sigma quality control and systems-driven approach, helps students create, communicate, and commercialize ideas. They learn to fail fast and cheap and master the art of rapid cycle problem solving. Says Eureka! Inventing's Hall, "Most companies left to their own device will produce stuff that's very similar to what they already do. Our goal is to interrupt that cycle and give them the courage through our coaching and our system to try and break that cycle."

Hall's comment underscores the key to figuring out how much process for unlocking creativity you really need at your company—it comes down to one question.

How tolerant is your company's culture to entertaining new ideas and the risk that comes with so doing?

At Taco Bell, they employ more than a mere tolerance of creative new ideas and risk-taking—it's part of their DNA.

Hall helps companies that have fear of failure and intolerance of risk/experimentation ingrained in their culture. Process helps give such clients confidence that the efforts will lead to a useable and justifiable output. It enables checkpoints and gives courage while taking participants through "scary steps" of innovating one at a time.

So size up where your company is on the spectrum and experiment with the amount of process and systems needed accordingly.

• *Turn off your self-monitoring brain*—Brain research supports the fact that creative people are able to block the instinct to judge their output when they're in the middle of being creative.

A researcher at Johns Hopkins University asked jazz musicians and rap artists to improvise a piece on the fly, while their brain was under the watchful scan of MRI (magnetic resonance imaging). The study revealed that while the artists were riffing, the part of their brain that is known to be the judging, self-monitoring part was virtually shut down. As the study noted, "For many activities it is important to have high self-monitoring of your behavior so that you don't say everything you think or do everything that you consider. But when you are generating new ideas, this function gets in the way."[7]

So, to spark your creativity, just let the ideas flow and be cognizant when the judging part of your inner dialogue starts kicking in.

Note that this willingness to let the ideas flow freely is even more important than the actual amount of effort you're putting into it. Inspiration researchers Thrash and Elliot studied a series of writing samples from college students that were judged for creativity by fellow students. They found that writers producing content judged to be more creative were more efficient and productive, spending less time pausing and more time writing. Those who exerted more effort spent more time pausing, deleted more words, and were better graded on technical merit, but their work wasn't considered more creative.[8]

Lastly on this front, don't be stingy with the number of ideas you're generating when you're thinking creatively. University of California psychology professor Dean Keith Simonton, an expert on creativity and innovation, says: "Many people succeed at producing innovations because they churn out a very large number of ideas, both good and bad. The most successful people tend to be those with the most failures."[9]

By that standard then I'm basically Bill Gates.

- *A word on brainstorming*—When thinking of techniques for opening up creativity, most people tend to go straight to brainstorming. Creativity expert David Burkus reminds us, however, that brainstorming is just one step in a larger creative process. Says Burkus,

Researchers have developed a variety of different models of creativity, from the Osborn-Parnes creative problem-solving method to design thinking. What all of these methods share are some common stages, of which brainstorming is only one. Before divergent thinking can have any benefit, your team needs to have thoroughly researched the problem and be sure their brainstorming answers the right question. Afterward, divergent thinking should be followed up with convergent thinking, where ideas are combined and sorted out to find the few answers that might be the best fit so that they can be prototyped, tested, and refined. But if your entire creative method is to get your team into a room and fill up a whiteboard, you're missing out.[10]

So brainstorming has its place—just know there's a bigger storm of important activity that should surround it.

Environment

- *Carve out the right space and time*—This two-pronged piece of advice for unleashing creativity was one of the most common themes I heard from my Creative Board of Directors. First, the need to create a space where a team can go to dream and create is essential. And the more unusual the space itself or the way the space is made to feel, the better.

  The research of scientist Christina Fong at Carnegie Mellon University indicates that employees who believe they're in an unusual environment can show increased creative thinking. Scott Barry Kaufman, a scientific director at the University of Pennsylvania, gives an example:

  Highly innovative companies such as Disney and IDEO are well aware of this dynamic, as their employees benefit from such unusual working environments. IDEO's workplace in Palo Alto, California has airplanes and bicycles suspended from the ceiling, plastic beaded curtains used as doors, and Christmas tree lights on display all year round. Everywhere you go are toys, gadgets, and prototypes from past projects. Indeed, multiple psychological studies suggest that a crucial trigger of creativity is the experience of unusual and unexpected events. Unexpected events can certainly mix emotions, and mixed emotions, as Fong has shown, can increase sensitivity to unusual associations and ideas.[11]

If at all possible, the space should be removed from day-to-day distractions—in a location where you can drown out all the other noise that clogs the brain on a typical workday. The literal ability to drown out other noise is why so many of us do some of our best thinking and dreaming in the shower. Research indicates that there's a scientific reason for this. As the comforting feel and enveloping sound of hot water flowing drowns everything else out, it helps the body and mind reach a state of relaxation and helpful distraction.[12] Plus your rendition of "Sweet Caroline" sounds *so* money.

Even more important than corralling or crafting a distraction-free space is carving out the time to use it. In fact, research indicates that the most discerning factor for companies considered top-tier for innovation and creativity (versus also-rans) is whether or not *they hold the time for creativity sacred.*

That means that nothing takes precedence in that moment over the need to get ideas flowing and to create. Not your boss's failure to plan, which caused your crisis, not an upcoming visit (aka inspection) from an executive officer, not mundane lead team meeting #3,442.

Nothing.

So try to pick a time that's most likely to be free from such distractions, and protect it with ferocity. Or think of the advice author Todd Henry shared with me: "Organizations must realize they can't be in perpetual harvest mode. It can't always be harvest season. There has to be a season for planting seeds."

Think of time carved out for creative thinking as the critical planting season, and then watch the fruits of your labor grow.

- *Form creative coalitions*—I lost count of the number of interviewees who described their company as risk averse, not really open to creativity and new ideas.

No doubt this is a difficult environment in which to fly your freak-flag (i.e., get creative). Todd Henry stresses the importance in such scenarios of forming creative coalitions, little outposts of side channel conversations that challenge the status quo and that encourage exploration of new ideas. These little bubbles of freedom can be extremely effective for keeping a spirit of creativity alive, even in a less-than-encouraging atmosphere.

And here's the key for a coalition working in such conditions (warning, this requires a bit of bravery): Keep taking permission to advance what's being developed, until that permission is taken away. By the way, if it's a truly compelling idea, odds are permission won't actually get taken away.

The point not to be missed here, though, is that creating the conditions and having the drive to be creative (thus inviting inspiration back in) is ultimately up to you and your personal leadership. This Anti-Muse nets a following of stagnancy that requires leadership to overcome.

Another important point is that when you can create your own little environment conducive to creativity, it's one of the keys to actual creative success (as opposed to how creative you believe you are, per se).

In fact, former Apple designer Mark Kawano dispels the myth that Apple's creative and design prowess is born primarily from its staff of world-class creative brains. Instead, he attributes it to the environment that Apple creates for nurturing new ideas and innovative approaches—everyone, across all functions, pays homage to the importance of ideas, creativity, and design that delights the end user. Kawano explains that this is why many Apple designers who leave Apple don't enjoy the same success they did at Apple—the conducive environment is absent in their new endeavor. Those same designers suddenly find themselves fighting for a seat at the table or fending off corporate grunts who want to prioritize a mundane metric over the hallowed user experience.[13]

You too can create the right kind of creativity-conducive atmosphere, even if on a more micro-level than Apple.

- *Surround yourself with supporters*—Restarting your creative engines can be daunting because it involves exposing yourself to the risk that others will reject your new ideas. Taking that risk in the presence of negative people exponentially magnifies that risk, as negative Nellies are so quick to suck the life out of new ideas and make the sharer feel rebuffed.

  So what to do?

  Ditch the discouragers. Surround yourself with people who are positive minded and receptive to your creative overtures. Rekindling anything is hard enough, so you want to add sparks, not a wet blanket. If you want to experience the wet blanket effect, invite Al Gore to the grand-opening of an SUV factory.

- *Sweat the team composition*—The standard opening piece of advice on creating a maximally creative team is to stock it with creative, divergent thinkers.

  Duh.

  You're going to have to work harder than that.

  More important than divergence is deliberateness. That is, being deliberate about who is on the team, what the right mix of experiences and experience levels is, and how big the team is.

  Research findings on all of these fronts may surprise you.

  The immediate assumption by many is to go for as diverse a team as possible. However, London Business School professor Lynda Gratton offers up a surprising caution based on her research. Says Gratton:

  > Diversity also creates problems. Our research shows that team members collaborate more easily and naturally if they perceive themselves as being alike. The differences that inhibit collaboration include not only nationality but also age, educational level, and even tenure. Greater diversity also often means that team members are working with people that they know only superficially or have never met before— colleagues drawn from other divisions of the company, perhaps, or even from outside it. We have found that the higher the proportion of strangers on the team and the greater the diversity of background and experience, the less likely the team members are to share knowledge or exhibit other collaborative behaviors.[14]

  So while some diversity in team composition is a must, ensure that there are enough threads of commonality to bolster overall collaboration levels.

As for team size, Gratton, in line with other researchers, has found that smaller is better. In fact, her research showed that after a team expanded beyond twenty people, the tendency to collaborate markedly decreases.[15] (Although your Super Bowl betting squares are easier to sell.)

Once you're under twenty members in team size, any number of teammates can yield equally creative output; it's more dependent on the next variable—the characteristics of individual team members.

The four most critical characteristics of individuals on a team considered to be highly creative are: (1) passion, (2) productivity, (3) collaboration, and (4) technical skill (competence in their job to be able to effectively contribute).[16]

So if you're given a chance to recruit your team for inducing creativity, keep all of the above in mind. If the team you've got is the team you've got, at least model passion, productivity, and collaboration to help bring along your counterparts.

Mindset

- *Don't talk about building it, build it*—A key part of getting creativity going is to well, just get it going.

  You might have heard of Facebook's "Hackathons," the dusk 'til 6 a.m. sessions where engineers build prototypes for a pet idea, as long as it's outside their day job. What's inspiring about that is just how ingrained the prototyping mindset is at Facebook. Dubbed "The Hacker Way," it's about creatively solving a problem using the means you have at your disposal. As one company guidebook says, "It's a prison shiv, not a Ginsu knife. MacGyver, not Bond." It's also about do, don't ask. Just build it. Test. Learn. Iterate. And it's a driver of Facebook's product development success.

  So build it, and they will come.

Or maybe they won't.

Yet.

But at least you'll have gotten things off the ground and creativity flowing.

- *Never follow*—A great way to unlock creativity is to force its hand. Imagine if you adopted the mindset of the Taco Bell team. Chief Food Innovation Officer Matthews told me that the entire mindset is to never, ever follow. By definition, this requires a spirit of experimenting and always trying creative new things. The executive team never holds the broader team back. In fact, just the opposite—it encourages constant evolution.

  Applying even a bit of this spirit to your business will knock complacency on its can, which is a common barrier to creativity. As Todd Henry puts it, "Entrenchment is not an effective strategy for being creative and inspired."

  Here's another way to think about it. As a leader, I never forget this personal mantra about the talent I bring onto my team:

  Don't hire eagles then ask them to fly in formation.

  Inspiring leaders don't do this.

  Leaders looking to unleash the best don't do this.

  People who are inspired don't fly in formation. They chart their own course. And so they soar.

  You can too.

  Break formation.

- *Ask questions*—One of the surest ways to spark creativity is to simply ask questions—a lot of them. That includes asking "What if?" before asking "How?" Insatiable curiosity is the order of the day.

  Jason Kotecki, creativity expert and author of *Penguins Can't Fly* (in which he humorously questions rules that don't exist), encourages you to be childlike, not childish, in your unending curiosity. He encourages you not to accept everything you see. Especially all the unwritten rules we tend to live by that Kotecki warns us about, like thou shalt get thine in-box to zero, thou shall wait for permission, or thou shalt care what other people think.[17]

Or thou shalt actually read the greeting card before signing it.

OK, that last unwritten rule was mine.

Anyway, the net here is that asking questions challenges assumptions, which reveals opportunities, which unlocks creativity.

And that's an unwritten rule you actually should follow (sorry Mr. Kotecki).

- *Be willing to do the hard work of creativity and innovation*— Kotecki framed this mindset for me this way:

> Unlocking creativity is like fishing. To catch a fish, you need to be committed enough to just sit there and fish as long as it takes. Once in a great while, a fish will actually jump in your boat. With creativity, you need to be disciplined enough to just sit in that boat and create, and then inspiration comes. Once in a while, you'll be walking around town and an idea will just emerge, that's like the fish jumping into the boat, and you're thankful for it. But really, if you're going to sit in the boat without a pole and wait for the fish to jump in the boat, good luck with that. You're much better off to put the time in with the pole every day.

Harvard Business School professor Linda Hill takes it a step further by defining the hardest work of all in unleashing creativity and innovation, specifically for a team. Hill defines it as managing the paradox that "leaders need to *unleash* individuals' talents, yet also *harness* all those diverse talents to yield a useful and cohesive result."[18]

It's this combination of unleashing the joy of creating and guiding that creativity to a productive outcome that most completely ushers inspiration back in.

Hill goes on to identify six paradoxes of *unleashing* and *harnessing* a team's creativity and innovation (six things that must be balanced):[19]

1. Affirm each person's need to be individually recognized for creative contributions while ensuring that team needs for such acknowledgement aren't subjugated.
2. Encourage a supportive energy among team members for new ideas while still advocating healthy debate.
3. Foster a continuous learning environment as new ideas are explored while still expecting high performance.
4. Champion improvisation of new ideas while having enough structure in place to progress the idea.
5. Show a mix of patience and sense of urgency with the development of new ideas.
6. Ensure a mixture of bottom-up creative initiatives (led by the troops) and top-down interventions (for the troops).

Doing the hard leadership work of managing these paradoxes is an imperative if you want to unleash maximally productive creativity for you and your team. As Hill put it, "Leaders who 'live' on the Harness side will never fully unleash the 'slices of genius' in their people; those who always stay on the Unleash side will have constant chaos and never solve any problems for the collective good."[20]

• *Keep going when most others don't*—Eureka! Inventing's Hall says he's seen firsthand that companies known as great innovators have an astounding secret to their success.

They keep going.

They are persistent in working through the problem at hand to come up with creative solutions. Hall says so many companies don't succeed in creative ventures simply because they give up.

Ever notice how often it happens that when you're working really hard to solve a problem and you step away from it for a while, and you go think about anything else, then come back to the problem, that the solution then quickly begins to materialize?

Your subconscious needs time to process. That means walking away from a problem and coming back to it—over and over if necessary.

Hollywood director/producer Montgomery tells of an old creative cohort of his who used to say, "It only takes a minute to come up with a good idea—I just don't know when in the next month I'll have it."

The point here is that creativity is often born from perseverance.

And from the ingenuity you conjure up when others have given up.

As Montgomery told me, "Creativity is resourcefulness in solving problems."

Your resourcefulness should contradict history at times. It should blow off the know-it-alls. It should be driven by a fierce belief that your creative solution will help your business win again (or stay winning).

Resourcefulness will reward you with the best idea, which is never the easiest idea.

This Anti-Muse that hides our paints on us to revel in a blank canvas is sooo over. And you're sooo under no obligation to pay her any mind anymore.

It's time to create a masterpiece. Or a mess, for now.

Who cares which one?

Just create—and elevate.

9

Insignificance
(REFORMULATED)

HOW'S THIS FOR a virtuous cycle? Imbuing your work with greater significance and meaning energizes you and attracts more such energy in the form of inspiration. Achieving an inspired state nets higher levels of meaning, which yields still more energy and inspiration, as research indicates.[1]

Not too bad.

Oh, and one other thing if you inject more significance into your work.

You'll live longer.

Research conducted for the book *The Longevity Project*, by Dr. Howard Friedman, revealed a fascinating conclusion. Turns out the advice to slow down, take it easy, and retire in a relaxing location is bad advice in terms of longevity of life (although it's great for Florida real estate). The research indicated that those who live the longest are those who work hard the longest, and do so on things personally meaningful to them. As Dr. Friedman put it,

"The responsible and successful achievers thrived in every way, especially if they were dedicated to things and people beyond themselves."[2]

Suffice it to say that the stakes are high for vanquishing the Anti-Muse of Insignificance.

However, research shows that we're facing an unprecedented surge in feelings of insignificance, a fact vastly exacerbated by our 24/7 access to a global infotainment network, where we're constantly exposed to the success stories and accomplishments of celebrities. It creates an unrealistic and irrelevant comparison base of the most "significant" individuals in the world, to which we can't stop comparing ourselves.[3]

So, we more and more start from a base of feeling inadequate, like me at a Chippendale's show.

Now, what about the work that our inadequate selves are doing every day? A Towers Watson Global Study showed that almost 40 percent of employees don't even understand how their work contributes to accomplishing the organization's business goals,[4] let alone feeling like their work is making an impact.

Whoa.

We've got work to do.

Take heart though. You can bring back a greater sense of significance to your work with what follows. I offer time-tested, research-backed veins of impact you can mine to bring greater significance to your work—presented as a series of case studies.

Think of these as a set of significance boosters or a collection of mantras for leaving your mark.

And remember, impact invites inspiration.

LEAD WHAT ONLY YOU CAN LEAD

And that means even if it's difficult. Ask yourself what you're uniquely suited to lead or what unique contribution you could make—whether due to your position in the organization or based on your skills and passions. Know what your "superpowers" are and commit to using those extreme strengths to make things worth happening, happen. Odds are, by the way, you'll intuitively recognize what simply must be, and can only be, led by you.

It's up to you to turn your intuition into an imprint.

Take the case of the late Nora Ephron.

Most know Ephron as an Academy Award–nominated screenwriter and director of such classic films as *Sleepless in Seattle, You've Got Mail,* and *Silkwood* (I believe *Sharknado* as well—but I could be wrong).

Many know of Ephron as queen of the quips, a sharp and funny woman who said of her internship at the White House in 1961, "It has become horribly clear to me that I'm probably the only young woman who ever worked in the Kennedy White House whom the President did not make a pass at."[5]

Not as many know that Ephron had a plan to lead things of meaning that only she could lead.

In her 1996 Wellesley College commencement address she noted that women of her generation weren't expected to do much of anything.[6] And yet Ephron set a standard for how successful women could be, in as many careers as they wanted.

She started her career as a wildly successful journalist and used that first standard-shaking breakthrough to do more of the same. Ephron would go on to become a successful essayist, novelist, blogger, playwright, and producer in addition to her brilliant screenwriting career.

Leveraging such phenomenal widespread success, she set out to become a director—one who could yet again serve as a role model for women trying to break into male-dominated industries. But more important, she knew that becoming a director would give her a powerful platform. She could use this platform to create roles for women as important and interesting as those that men regularly get—a struggle that still rages in Hollywood today.

As Ephron herself put it in a documentary about screenwriters breaking into Hollywood:

It's a very male business. Vast portions of it . . . might as well be the United States Army in 1943. Most directors, I discovered, need to be convinced that the screenplay they're going to direct has something to do with them, and this is a tricky thing if you write screenplays where women have parts that are equal to or greater than the male part. . . .You look at a list of directors and it's all boys; it certainly was when I started as a screenwriter. So I thought, I'm just going to become a director and that'll make it easier.[7]

Publicly, and privately, Nora Ephron made a life of leading things she knew she was in a unique position to lead. It became known later in her life that she put tremendous energy into mentoring women (and men) to achieve greatness in a multi-pronged way. She mentored women like actress, writer, producer, and director Lena Dunham, and did so even while she was quietly fighting an illness that would ultimately take her life.[8]

Ephron knew of her responsibility to use her unique talents to lead, without excuse. As she closed out her Wellesley commencement address, "Above all be the heroine of your life, not the victim."[9]

Shards of glass ceilings are still strewn everywhere today because Nora Ephron led what she knew she uniquely could.

WORK ON A SYSTEM VERSUS IN A SYSTEM

One of the ways to do more work of significance is to lead changes that make an impact on a workplace's systems or the way work gets done.

It's good when you make solid contributions working *in* the system and improving the smell of the place. But it's significant when you lead unexpected contributions working *on* the system that change the DNA of the place.

Tony Hsieh, CEO of Zappos (the online shoe giant), decided to work on the entire system for how a company is organized rather than work in the traditional system.

At Zappos, the standard idea of having a boss and a hierarchy has been blown up and replaced by a flatter organization that's organized by work charts, not org charts. The radical experiment is called a holacracy.

This means that the traditional idea of having a boss is history at Zappos. (So wait, if you work there, now what do you do with your "World's #1 Boss" mug you keep your pencils in?)

Work is divided up into a vast variety of work circles, and each employee can choose among the work circles to create their own work plans. Bosses are called "lead links" who help facilitate who works on what, but they have very little formal authority anymore—they're facilitators.

Harvard Business School professor Ethan Bernstein described holacracy this way:

> If a traditional organization is like a prix-fixe restaurant, where you just walk in and get an Italian meal (as a set course), they're now giving their employees the chance to select all the different roles, the appetizer, the main course, the dessert, on a fairly regular basis on the assumption that that's the sort of individual who will help Zappos succeed in the future. That, I think, has a lot of logical sense, especially in a world that's increasingly in need of adaptability, which we know comes from the front line and from workers being engaged.[10]

Wow.

I've had weird dreams of taking away power from a jerk boss and watching him freak out at the realization that we'd become "equals." You know, *Twilight-Zone* stuff.

But Zappos actually did it.

The gambit is designed to increase self-management, adaptability, and productivity, as people's passions more greatly align with what they want to work on. Zappos believes they will ultimately gain competitive advantage through this new way of being organized.

There is no shortage of doubters, even within Zappos. In 2015, the company experienced a whopping *29 percent turnover* as employees who found the new system too confusing chose to leave.[11]

But Zappos founder Hsieh remains steadfast that self-management is the organization of the future, and even re-upped his commitment to the concept in a 4,300 word memo to his employees in 2015. In the memo, he referenced the work of consultant Frederic Laloux and his book *Reinventing Organizations*. In the book Laloux color codes companies based on their organizational structure approach. Orange is a traditional top-down structure like Walmart, green is for more evolved organizations like Starbucks, and teal is the color for the next stage of development, "self-management, bringing one's whole self to work, and having a purpose beyond making money."[12]

Hsieh went all-in on teal.

It ultimately remains to be seen how successful the effort is, but no one doubts how significant it is. Success could spawn reapplication and change the face of management as we know it today.

At least until the robots take over and we're all reporting to them in an astonishing return of hierarchy.

The good news is that you don't have to take on the entire way your organization is organized. Just organize an effort to work on a system, any system, that begs for improvement instead of accepting the current system at face value.

BE THE CHAMPION FOR CHANGE SORELY NEEDED

I talked in the previous section about leading change on a work process or accepted system for doing things. Here I refer to the more general idea of leading any change sorely needed.

When Bill Sandbrook took the job as CEO of U.S. Concrete, the need for change was everywhere. The stock was trading at under $2 per share, employee morale was terrible, and headquarters and the selling and manufacturing force were often at odds.

The concrete company was crumbling.

Fast forward to this writing, where the stock has risen a meteoric 2,400 percent since Sandbrook took over in 2011.

What happened?

No, he didn't launch gluten-free concrete.

Sandbrook made himself the champion for change sorely needed, often in unconventional ways.

The Army veteran and Wharton grad told me he entered the job with a healthy disdain for the widely practiced 100 day plan, calling it hogwash "because you come in believing your own b.s." He first took the time to carefully evaluate the change needed, and then executed accordingly. He moved the company's headquarters to shake up the culture and reframed HQ's role. As Sandbrook told me, "HQ doesn't make any money; the ones selling/manufacturing in the field do."

And yet HQ viewed the field as an impediment and had made itself a controlling gate. Need brakes for a truck or a gear reducer for a conveyor belt? Clear it with HQ first.

That changed.

The role of HQ was redefined to that of being an enabler that served the field, not the other way around.

Sandbrook instituted many other cultural changes needed, like making empowerment and accountability the standard and banning PowerPoint presentations to keep everyone focused on progressing a project versus looking good in a meeting.

I've experienced this myself in the corporate world, where people were more afraid of a bad meeting than a bad result. These were the same people who timed their bathroom breaks with the boss's to get more face time.

Sandbrook also made changes in how the CEO interacted with employees, like being effusive even with small wins and stating that while giving employees more money was nice, what really counted was to create more meaning for them every day they came to work.

Making change sorely needed isn't only for the C-Suite.

You'll see how sweet it is when you do the same. (See what I did there?)

HELP SOLVE A CIRCUMSTANCE

Think of the last time you were in a real pickle and someone went out of their way to help you out.

You don't forget that.

Rolling up your sleeves and really digging in to help someone in a predicament is a guaranteed way to make a real impact. Be in tune to when such an opportunity arises and be ready to invest some of your time and energy.

Susan Jenkins most certainly was.

I met the seasoned nurse in a coffee shop in Vancouver while working on this very book and happened to strike up a conversation with her. I even took off my headphones to do so.

She was in the midst of reading a letter from a former patient that had brought tears to her eyes, thus prompting my entry into conversation.

Jenkins told me the patient was thanking her for going above and beyond to help her out of a major circumstance. The nurse and patient had become close friends, which led to the patient's confession that her medical bills had caught up with her. She had already tapped out every source of medical aid she could find and was now faced with the likely foreclosure of her home, the selling off of most of her worldly assets, and the required compromise (in a number of ways) of her son's well-being.

Jenkins had spotted a major opportunity to help someone out of a circumstance.

She personally conducted a fund-raiser to help the patient out. The fund-raiser, enhanced by the credibility of a nurse, raised enough money to help her friend save her home and avoid other unwanted compromises.

While that's an amazing enough outcome, what really amazed me was the impact helping to solve such a circumstance had on the nurse.

As she told me:

I've been a bit checked out at work lately, if I'm honest. I'm in a place where the amount of nurse empowerment is going in the wrong direction. But knowing that I can find unique circumstances in which I can play a role in helping solve problems for others has renewed my energy. I've found a way to matter more. I guess you could say I'm refueled and on the hunt for more circumstances to help solve—not just with patients, but with peers, family, and friends.

Try going on a similar search. Significance won't be far behind.

FILL AN UNMET NEED OR DO A DEED THAT NEEDS DOING

Serial entrepreneur Blake Mycoskie was traveling through Argentina and enjoying total immersion in its culture when he noticed something.

Everywhere he turned, there they were.

He saw them being worn in every city he went to, in night-clubs, cafés, on every corner. Even farmers were wearing them.

No, not Mom jeans.

Simple canvas shoes that the locals called alpargatas.

Always the entrepreneur, the idea struck Mycoskie that this comfortable shoe might go over well in America. But because he was on break and resting from the demands of a current start-up, he just tucked the idea away and went back to his vacation.[13]

Probably for the best because it would have been just one more basic shoe idea among the thousands of ideas discerning shoe buyers see every day. I've never been confused for Louis Vuitton, but I'm guessing it likely would have been quickly squashed.

But the story doesn't end there.

Toward the end of his trip he met an American woman who was organizing a shoe drive for the thousands upon thousands of children in the area who couldn't afford shoes. Mycoskie tagged along and over the next several days saw firsthand the problem that a lack of shoes created for children. No shoes meant extreme exposure to illness and the inability to attend school—not to mention the discomfort of blisters, scrapes, and cuts.[14]

The deed that needed doing burst up through the clouds of dust that clogged the dirty streets to reveal itself.

Blake Mycoskie was going to sell those alpargatas after all.

However, with a profound twist, one that many hail as the true beginning of social entrepreneurism.

For every pair of canvas shoes he'd sell, he'd give one away to a child in need. You buy a pair today, they get a pair tomorrow. Tomorrow's Shoes. TOMS.[15]

Today, TOMS sells over half a billion dollars in shoes but, much more important, has put shoes on the feet of over 60 million children. The "One for One" social business model has been expanded to TOMS eyewear, coffee, and bags to enable better eyesight, safer drinking water, and safe birthing kits.[16]

More than 100 other "One for One" businesses have sprung up since then, and Mycoskie has taken a vast amount of his personal wealth accumulated from the success of TOMS to create a seed fund to invest in more such social-minded businesses.

All because he saw an unmet need, a deed that needed doing.

You can do the same in the exotic locale of your own workplace.

Keep asking yourself, "What glaring need remains unmet?" "What deed needs doing?" and the opportunity for more significance will present itself to you as well.

REIMAGINE THE CATEGORY YOU COMPETE IN

The title of World's Fastest Man is cool enough by itself.

Placing first in a series of high-pressure races, over and over, has surely earned Usain Bolt that moniker.

And yet, upon closer examination, Bolt has not achieved the iconic status he now enjoys simply because he's been impossibly good in the impossibly difficult category of world-class sprinting.

For most every other human being on the planet, dominance in such a singularly compelling physical feat would be enough.

But Usain Bolt doesn't see it that way.

Bolt doesn't even see himself as in the sport of sprinting (even though he runs faster than your Internet connection).

He's reimagined who he is and what he does, viewing himself instead in the category of entertainment. Throughout his sprinting days, while Bolt talked often about wanting to win, he talked just as much about his desire to provide entertainment for his fans. This desire informed the way Bolt went about his races—waving to fans, laughing, touching as many hands as he could, taking countless selfies with fans, striking his famous "To Di World" or Thunderbolt pose for all. He turned his sprints into an event to entertain and celebrate his beloved country and fans.

By the way, he's entertained his way to an estimated net worth of over $60 million[17] and has parlayed his fame and fortune into leverage to give back to his beloved country of Jamaica in a variety of ways.[18]

What is the business you compete in? How might you reframe, expand, and reimagine the category in which it lies?

Ask yourself, "What business am I really in?" Tide detergent decided years ago that they're not in the laundry detergent business; they're in the clothing-care business. Special K decided that they're not in the cereal business; they're in the healthy-lifestyle business.

You can redefine something by thinking broader, reinventing an end user benefit, or by imagining doing something that your competitors would be afraid you were doing—just to mention a few ways.

If something as straightforward as "run as fast as you can in a straight line for 100 meters" can be reimagined, you can find your own source of significance by reimagining just about anything.

HELP MOVE SOMEONE FORWARD

Facebook COO and author of *Lean In*, Sheryl Sandberg, has started an entire movement of helping move someone forward—particularly women helping other women move forward. She launched an initiative called *Together Women Can*, enrolling a host of celebrities and others to help advance the cause. Sandberg said of the effort, "So many women are lending their voices to this campaign because they have benefited firsthand from the support of other women and know what a difference it can make."[19]

Arianna Huffington has weighed in on the effort too, saying "The support I've received from women, both personally and professionally, has shown me over and over again the importance of creating what I call a tribe—people who will always be in your corner, always there for you, in good times and tough times, whether you're succeeding or failing."[20]

Female or male, what a powerful thought of significance—joining someone's tribe as a passionate member with the goal of helping them excel.

Note that I'm starting a tribe for myself too, because it takes a village. So, I guess I'm asking you to be one of my Village People.

BECOME AN EXPERT OTHERS TURN TO

Scott Stratten makes over a million dollars a year just by talking.

As of this writing Stratten is one of the hottest keynote speakers in the country, in demand as a sought-after expert on what *not* to do in the world of marketing and sales. He has a popular podcast called *The UnPodcast: The Business Podcast for the Fed-Up* as well as bestselling books titled *UnMarketing* and *UnSelling*, in which he rails on what's wrong with these disciplines, often pointing out specific case studies of failure. He writes a blog titled the *UnBlog* and advertises as a keynoter who does *UnSpeaking*. Notice a theme here?

Stratten will be the first to admit that he's no expert on how to fix all the things that are wrong; he's just an expert on what's wrong—and shares this insight in a very humorous and engaging manner.

And people are listening.

People don't just turn to Stratten for his expertise—they typically pay $20,000 per engagement to get it. For perspective, the National Speakers Association considers its members to be full-fledged professional speakers once they hit $25,000 in annual speaking revenue.

That's a decent *week* for Stratten.

Stratten told me with great passion that he's resisted the pull to go off in many directions in pursuit of even greater revenue. All his work funnels into a simple business model; everything enables more speaking gigs—gigs that put his expertise on display and that have a real impact on the way people view his subject matter.

As Stratten told me: "I have two responsibilities. Kill it on stage for my client and stay on top of my industry so I can speak intelligently."

He works hard to always have something relevant, useful, and, yes, significant, to say on the platform he's worked so hard to create.

And as outspoken as Stratten is, the results of his "be expert at being an expert" business model is the one thing that speaks for itself.

You can build your own platform of significance too. Sharpen your expertise on a topic of passion and share it so well that others seek you out for the value you provide.

PURSUE A PURPOSE AND A LEGACY

No one could ever say Dana Vollmer wasn't driven.

The 2016 Olympic women's swimming gold medalist couldn't have possibly achieved that honor without intense drive.

But there was more at work here than just an insane work ethic.

Seventeen months prior to winning that gold medal, Dana Vollmer did something that no one believed she could recover from in time to compete at the Olympics (let alone win a gold medal).

She had a baby.

Then, seventeen months later, she won a gold medal.

For perspective, it takes me seventeen months to get around to putting the garden hose away.

This incredible and incredibly significant feat took more than just hard work to pull off. It took a sense of purpose and the desire to leave a legacy behind. This was Vollmer's secret weapon that would lead her to astonish the world.

Vollmer encapsulated her sense of purpose and desired legacy in a hashtag that went viral: #MommaOnAMission. This rallying cry started as an expression of her desire to get back in shape after having her baby. But it would grow to take on so much more meaning for her as her journey back to competitive swimming progressed.

As Vollmer told me, "The hashtag is also about learning the little ways you can get wins along the way in your journey. It's a feeling that moms are so much stronger than any of us knew that they were. It's about taking on the challenge of having a baby, yes, but also about loving the joy that the child brings into your life."

It was also an expression of Vollmer's sense of purpose: #MommaOnAMission reminded her to be a role model for other new moms. She could inspire them to enjoy the new journey and all of the challenges it would bring, and to know that they could get to wherever they wanted to go after having a child.

It would be a fitting legacy. A worthy purpose. An inspiring mission possible.

Something of true significance.

You should be intentional about identifying and articulating your legacy and purpose too (my book *Make It Matter* helps you with this).

Doing so will give you Olympic drive and help drown any sense of insignificance.

INSPIRE SOMEONE

It happened about fifteen years ago.

I was at a crossroads in my career. Things were going well enough. I was progressing up the food chain fairly rapidly and enjoying increased responsibility and all the associated perks.

But something was missing.

Other than my car keys again, I mean.

I kept coming back to the same set of questions. "What am I *really* working so hard for?" "Why am I missing so many hours away from my loved ones?" "Surely this has to be about more than selling 10 percent more widgets than I did last year?"

"What's the point?"

I found myself scrambling at an ever-accelerating pace to find any sense of significance in the work I was doing.

Right about that time I got promoted.

Terrific! Surely, that was what I was working so hard for. More money, more power, more stature.

All that was great except for one problem.

I didn't care.

And I thought I would. But the high of the promotion wore off in about two days, and the sense of dread moved back from the peripheral into plain view once again.

It was at that point that I began a period of deep introspection. Examining what really mattered to me, what my values were, what made my heart and mind sing. Many of the same types of powerful self-questions I share in *Make It Matter*. I was starting to make progress on identifying places where I could create more significance when an event kicked it into overdrive.

I saw a clip of Fred Rogers, the personality behind the long-running *Mister Rogers' Neighborhood* show, accepting a lifetime achievement award on the Daytime Emmys. Instead of droning on about all the people to thank, Rogers simply asked the audience for ten seconds of silence to consider someone in their lives who helped them become who they are today. He even offered to keep the time on his watch—and did.

While the camera panned those in the audience with tears in their eyes, it hit me.

That was it.

I could reframe and reshape the work I did into a life of servitude. I could make a real difference in the lives of others by striving to inspire someone. Every day.

And so I committed to that thought in a big way. I had the term *Inspire Someone* etched on the back of my iPhone to serve as a daily reminder of the significance I could bring to my time here on earth. My license plate became NSPRSM1. I went all-in.

And it's made all the difference in the world.

I'm not trying to tell you that what I've chosen as a driving thought is any more noble than what anyone else would home in on. I'm not trying to tell you I even achieve that goal each day.

What I am trying to tell you is that the thought of trying to inspire someone, every day, gives me tremendous focus.

It gives me a breathtaking sense of significance when I do manage to achieve it.

You can gain such a sense of significance in this manner as well, if you choose it as a focal point.

My honest hope for you after reading this chapter is that your concern about the Anti-Muse of Insignificance just became insignificant.

Try taking a stroll down a few of the aforementioned avenues. I think you'll find a destination that really matters.

10

Lack of Evocation

(REDISCOVERED)

IT WOULD BE understandable if Henri Landwirth bailed on the hope of ever being inspired by anything again. The death camp survivor had seen humanity at its absolute worst, enduring horrors as a child that would jade even the strongest of us in irreparable ways.

Landwirth somehow managed to persevere through the atrocities, eventually fleeing to America where, with little to his name, he began work in the hotel industry. Years of hard work would ultimately lead Landwirth to move from clerk to night manager, then to manager, then to owner of a hotel in Orlando, Florida.

It was at that time that Landwirth was asked if he'd donate a hotel room for a very sick six-year-old girl named Amy who desperately wanted to see Disney World. Landwirth agreed, but the remainder of Amy's travel plans simply took too long to put into place.

Time ran out on Amy.

She succumbed to her leukemia before her wish could ever be filled.

Landwirth, heartbroken but determined, vowed that no child would ever be denied their wish to visit such a magical place—especially at a time when the child and family needed a special vacation the most.

And so, with help from the hospitality and tourism industry in Central Florida, Landwirth founded *Give Kids the World.* The charity now rests on a 79-acre resort with 144 villas for families in need, its own set of attractions, easy access to Disney World, and access granted within twenty-four hours when unfortunate circumstances require.[1]

Landwirth became deeply inspired, an evoked sense of inspiration born from his experience with Amy, a child he never got to meet.

Inspiration can indeed be externally evoked in all of us, fortunately without requiring such dire circumstances.

Even if you work in conditions such that you can't imagine anything *ever* inspiring you, it can indeed happen. Let's break down just how that might be so.

THE THREE CONDITIONS OF EVOCATION

Research indicates that three conditions must be present for an outside force to evoke inspiration in us, conditions all present in Landwirth's case and conditions that could just as likely occur for you, too.

Something evokes inspiration if it's disruptive (forces you to think about things differently), if it's relevant (to core human motives), and if it's attainable (feels like it can be accomplished).[2]

That's it—not exactly an impossible or improbable list.

Landwirth became aware that a terrible problem existed (ill children wanting to see Disney World but unable to do so), which spoke to core human motives to help (especially because he too had suffered trauma as a child), and which illuminated an attainable solution (creating the means to facilitate a magical family vacation).

Now, I realize that this is all well and good but the problem remains that these are conditions we have to wait for, correct? And the Lack of Evocation Anti-Muse would love nothing better than for you to wait around for such conditions, like a telemarketer waits until you're eating dinner.

But in truth, you don't have to wait and hope. We're going on the offensive against this offensive Anti-Muse.

THE THREE BEHAVIORS OF EVOCATION

There are three specific behaviors you can engage in that will greatly increase the likelihood that you'll be inspired by something (something disruptive, relevant, attainable). Let's look at each.

1. *Influencing the mood and the mix*—Let's start simple. You can elevate the mood of your environment by being positive, enthusiastic, and optimistic, which will greatly increase the likelihood that you'll receive the same in return. Positive environments and mindsets make it more likely you'll be inspired by something—plain and simple.

    You can also increase the quantity and mix of stimuli to potentially be inspired by when you go into seek mode (as discussed in Chapter 3, "Settling and Boredom [Rejected]"). Trying a variety of new experiences increases the likelihood that you'll strike a spark of inspiration.

2. *Studying the routine and the remarkable*—It might surprise you that I'm suggesting that you study things routine in nature so you can be inspired by something.

Well, it turns out that inspiration can be uncovered in things we take for granted.

Arkansas schoolteacher Martha Cothren did just this for her students in a most unusual way.

The students arrived on the first day of school to learn that their desks had been removed. They further discovered that the desks wouldn't reappear until one of the students could guess exactly what had to be done to earn those desks.

Cothren solicited answers at the end of each period throughout the day. Answers of "good grades" and "good behavior" turned out to be incorrect. By the end of the day, still no correct answer, and still no desks. Several television stations caught wind of this story and showed up for the answer at day's end. At that point, Cothren let twenty-seven war veterans into her class-room, each carrying a desk.

She then turned to her students and told them, "You don't have to earn those desks. These men already did. They went halfway around the world, giving up their education and interrupting their careers and families so you could have the freedom you have. No one charged you for your desk. But it wasn't really free. These guys bought it for you. And I hope you never forget it."[3]

And I doubt those children ever have. Inspiration evoked from something taken for granted.

We can take many things for granted in our lives—people, places, things, Pop Tarts.

By practicing *focused appreciation*, stopping to con-sider what's special about a person, place, or thing in our life, we can elicit inspiration.

This even applies to focused appreciation of every-day things of beauty that we take for granted. A walk in nature, a stroll through a quaint seaside village, or catching a sunset can all stir feelings of inspiration and create a desire to mimic that sense of awe in other parts of our life.

You can also evoke inspiration by gaining exposure to remarkable work, ideas, or people. Recall in Chapter 8, "Dearth of Creating (Reconstituted)," that I talked about advertising agency creatives who sought out remarkable new experiences via Broadway plays or at museums—all to be exposed to professional brilliance in hopes of catching a spark of inspiration. You can do your own version of this by attending similar venues, by going to industry conferences and award shows, by setting up a "gallery walk" of work being done by your competitors, or by reading industry magazines that review your industry's work.

The point is to create chances for inspiration to be evoked by experiencing great work.

Along with remarkable work, you can get exposure to remarkable people. Attach yourselves to people who always seem to be inspired by and passionate about something. Seek exposure to an inspiring leader or relevant role model and absorb the virtue of their actions and outcomes. Research shows that the important part here is to study an attainable role model, one whose level of success is within reach—otherwise it becomes merely deflating.[4]

That said, research also indicates that there's an exception to this.

You can also study a hero who has actually achieved a remarkable, unattainable level of success (exhibiting inspiring qualities along the way), but in an arena *not relevant* to your daily environment or aspirations. A study on the inspirational power of the superstar basketball player Michael Jordan showed that he has enormous inspirational power despite achieving prowess in a profession highly irrelevant to almost all of us. The study, conducted among college students, found that because Jordan's level of success was beyond the reach of nearly all the students, and because basketball is not relevant to most students' aspirations, the potential for demoralizing comparisons was minimized, thereby opening the students to fully appreciating Jordan's skills. Thus, the study concluded, "Once the student appreciates Jordan's competence, he or she becomes inspired to place greater priority on developing competence, assuming that he or she is able to translate Jordan's inspiring qualities into a personal goal that is relevant and of appropriate difficulty."[5]

So, studying the right superstars, and superstar bosses, can evoke inspiration.

But what happens when not only is there no inspirational leader in sight, but your direct manager or chain of command is thoroughly uninspiring? You might be thinking something along the lines of, "Building a portfolio of ways to fight back against the nine Anti-Muses is all well and good, but my highly lackluster boss will make it all for naught—he/she just saps my will to carry on."

This is a critical point, as a Towers Watson study indicated that when it comes to energizing and inspiring others "few things can have as much immediate impact as an effective relationship with one's direct manager."[6] And research shows that we want inspiration from our boss more than any other leadership characteristic.

But unfortunately, as I pointed out in Chapter 1, statistics indicate that you're hardly alone if you see your boss as a blockade to inspiration.

In fact, 75 percent of employees say their boss stresses them out.[7] Thirty percent of office workers report that they've deliberately scheduled their time off around their manager's vacation in order to spend less time around their boss.[8] Furthermore, one survey even showed that half of all workers would fire their boss if they could, and 30 percent would recommend their manager be seen by a workplace psychologist.[9]

Yikes. The jokes almost write themselves.

And while it's a fact that a "poor relationship with manager" is the number one reason people leave a company,[10] if they can't leave (for whatever reason) it also leads to people choosing to quit and stay.

So, yes, your boss can ruin everything, and we need to be realistic about the devastating effects such "leaders" can have on the appearance of any inspiration.

And while expanding your support network (mentors, peers, external relationships) can help offset the uninspiring impact your boss is having, it doesn't change the fact that you still have to work with that person every day.

The good news is that this is where "converting" mechanisms kick in so you don't have to just accept the current state of affairs with your boss. You can engage in tactics that not only keep the uninspiring leader from killing any glimmer of inspiration, but also convert him or her into an actual source of inspiration.

Seriously.

Here's how.

3. *Morphing your manager into a source of inspiration*—I want to address the fact that there are many types of bad bosses (micromanagers, credit-grabbers, never-pleasers, unpredictables, just to name a few), and that I won't be providing solutions for every variation.

The common denominator across every type, however, is that they all sap your inspiration in some way. So now, in a section worthy of its own, we'll focus on how to neutralize the draining impact of bosses' uninspiring actions while behaving ourselves in ways that can *evoke inspiring behaviors in return.*

How to Morph Your Manager into a Source of Inspiration

1. *Start with the Commandments of Coping.* Trying to convert a bad boss into a source of inspiration is an aggressive goal, so we first must set a neutralizing foundation. Before we convert any boss into anything, we have to keep you from killing them.

So, let's start with some basic coping mechanisms for dealing with difficult, inspiration-sapping bosses, what I call the "Commandments of Coping."

- *Realize this too shall pass*—Everyone has a bad boss from time to time. Successful people learn how to manage through it. You can't let their hang-ups hang you up and start affecting your work and well-being. I know, easier said than done, but it's an important starting point. Too many try to deal with a tough boss from an emotional place rather than a reflective place.
- *Know that no single situation, or person, defines you*—Stay true to your values and being the best version of yourself when working with a difficult boss. Maybe this boss will take your job away from you, or you'll leave it, but they can't take away who you are and what you stand for. Ever.
- *Don't shrink, or shirk*—Don't back down to a bad boss. Stand your ground with confidence and calm. And you can't shirk your responsibility for improving the relationship. Things won't change by complaining. It starts with *you*, so own your part in the relationship and what you could do better. Want to change it as much as you need to change it.
- *Resist the temptation to label*—Once you've categorized your boss as horrid, evil, etc., you're more likely to dismiss their better points and unfairly categorize all of their messy points. Applying labels to your boss makes you jump to conclusions about their actions and makes you close-minded, which doesn't help when you need

open-mindedness to effect change. If it helps, think of the bad boss as a difficult client that you simply must learn to work with.

- *Learn to read their moods and identify triggers*—This is the low-hanging fruit part of the equation. Knowing their moods (when you can approach them with what) and what sets them off can help you avoid inspiration-sapping encounters. You've got enough work ahead of you to get things in a better place; don't drive through red lights on your way there.

- *Seek to understand*—I can't emphasize enough how important this is. When you understand the why behind the behavior of a difficult boss, what to do about it becomes much more self-evident. Specifically, seek to understand what's important to them and why they're doing what they are—that is, their motivations. You have motivations behind your behaviors too. This is the "heavy-lifting" Commandment because the motivations won't always be obvious. But through enough observation and inquiry, you'll discover what's driving their behavior. If it's fundamental character flaws, then there's probably not much you can do to improve things. But if the tension is based on a set of explainable behaviors, such comprehension drives the ability to cope as well as connect, which brings us to the next part.

2. *Begin building bridges.* Having addressed the basics of coping, it's time to move on to connecting. Research shows that the most important factor for enabling bosses to ultimately inspire you is whether or not you've developed an emotional connection with them.[11]

I'm not asking you to be soulmates.

But you don't have to be cellmates, either.

Work can be better than that—and so can your relationship with your boss.

I know how hard this can be, especially if your boss is just an utter jackwagon.

But you have to at least try to own the relationship and make the effort to get to know and be sincerely interested in your manager. See them as a person, just like you, with emotions, aspirations, and insecurities. Accept the imperfections. Remember that they are human and that we're all just trying to do our best in this crazy world. See the best parts of them. Be a confidant if needed, compassionate if required. Strive to add your boss to a list of those you'd want to stay connected with down the road—even if it's a stretch. Such an approach will force you to see the good in your manager and increase the likelihood that an inspiring connection will be made.

3. *Amp up their advocacy.* It's one thing to do the basics of your job well, it's another to do your job so well that it inspires your boss to become a fierce advocate for you. Such advocacy can be inspiring in many ways.

So the question is, in what manner does your boss most want your greatness to show up? (Besides the obvious over-delivery of results, and on-time delivery of their dry cleaning.)

How can you carve out your value proposition in their eyes and be visibly valuable?

How can you cheat the law of averages by being great at the *right things?*

Research indicates that the behaviors that most often induce advocacy from one's manager are when:[12]

- You exhibit strong ownership of your work and consistently and independently take the initiative.
- You engender unswerving confidence that you've got things covered (your boss "knows that you know," that you'll follow through on what you say you'll do, and that you'll always exhibit accountability—without excuses).

- You consistently go above and beyond, and often think outside the scope of current projects.
- You beat snakes out of the grass (uncover issues) and have solutions in tow.
- You serve as a capacity expander for your boss; you create time for them and make their job easier (versus being a constant time-suck).
- You make an effort to make them look good—in a productive, not political, manner.

Again, upping your game on these fronts can't make up for a truly toxic, character-flawed manager. But practicing these behaviors will certainly increase the odds of inspiration-inducing advocacy.

4. *Encourage their investment in you.* Imagine how inspiring it would be if you had someone who was truly vested in your continued learning and growth, and took the time to invest in your education accordingly.

I asked Cincinnati Bengals head football coach Marvin Lewis what was the most fulfilling part of his job.

His answer?

No, not getting tons of "We're # 1" foam fingers for free.

"Helping others achieve their goals. It's why we all coach."

You would hope that all workplace managers would share this sentiment about their profession. But we're talking here about instances when your manager/coach doesn't delight in this as much, if at all.

You can enhance your bosses' desire to coach you through three actions in particular:

(a) invite them in and seek out feedback and advice, and then eagerly act on it, (b) continually demonstrate a natural curiosity and actively ask for learning and growth opportunities, and (c) show appreciation to your boss for their role in helping you learn, grow, and succeed.

These actions send the right message to your boss that their efforts will be worthy and worthwhile. In truth, very few people don't actually like helping others improve, so such an outcome will feed on itself and feed a healthier relationship.

5. *Flip the switch on the power of partnership.* This one is about inspiration through accomplishment—working in tandem and in tune with your boss to get important things done. There can be no question that making progress on things that matter is inspiring. To do so in partnership with your boss can be especially rewarding and first requires taking care of a few basic "housekeeping" items.

Start by getting crystal clear on expectations. Let their agenda drive yours for the time being—there's nothing wrong with that in the spirit of focus and partnership. As you build your relationship you can influence the agenda more and more over time (as I encourage you to do in Chapter 5, "Loss of Control [Reverted]").

As mentioned earlier, also seek to understand your boss's goals, motives, and triggers—what sets them off—so you understand the guardrails of working effectively with them.

With this framework of understanding complete, you can then move on to what most bosses believe are the most "partnership-like" practices an employee can engage in with them. Research reveals that these behaviors are:[13]

- Let the info flow: Bring your boss in early on things (including elevating issues quickly), keep them regularly informed, and avoid surprises and guns to the head for decisions.
- Adjust your preferences and work style if necessary to mesh with theirs. For example, Peter Drucker divides bosses into "readers" and "listeners." Some bosses like to get their information in written form, so they can study it quietly on their own, while others like information to be presented to them so they can process out loud with the presenter and ask clarifying questions.

- Anticipate your manager's needs and be reliable in delivering them.
- Pick your battles—lean heavily toward being cooperative (their job is hard enough).
- Be transparent in your needs—understand your boss is not psychic.
- Appreciate your boss's point of view and get that there's a lot to their job that you don't see.
- Have their back—always.

So practice these behaviors to do your part in fostering a great partnership.

6. *Bring the attitude you want reciprocated.* The role of attitude pops up again, as it did earlier in this chapter. If you're inspired, for example, by people who are positive-minded, are always looking to help you succeed and make you look good, and are always respectful, then act this way yourself. Do so especially with your boss.

We can't help but get caught up in the attitudes of those we most closely work with—good or bad.

And take special note of leaving insecurity and anxiety at the curb—it will push your manager away. As career expert Nicole Williams says, "Insecurity and anxiety don't just ruin romantic relationships."[14]

7. *Learn how to give your boss feedback.* There is no shortage of boss behaviors that employees find uninspiring. But the myriad of possible misbehaviors all have one thing in common: They will persist unless your boss understands the impact they are having. You can address this by giving your boss feedback.

Gulp.

No one relishes the thought of giving a boss feedback. But once you get some practice, it becomes easier.

First, of course, make sure your boss is open to it. If you aren't certain, ask. Frame it as you have some observations that could be helpful. Assuming you get a green light, proceed with bravery, reminding yourself of the importance of making sure your boss fully understands the impact his/her behaviors are having on you (and others).

The truth is, most dysfunctional bosses have no idea of the depth/extent of the negative impact their behavior might be having on you or the organization. Many would be horrified, but appreciative, to find out the realities of their behavior. So, I'm encouraging you to conduct an awareness campaign, and gently help them understand these realities. Show humility, transparency, and empathy in so doing.

Then, "the rules" are quite straightforward. Be respectful, direct, private, and specific as you give the feedback. Give examples that focus on the impact of their behavior, never making it about them as a person. Write the feedback down ahead of time so you aren't going off the cuff (and so you know just where to pour on the waterworks. Just kidding. Really. Don't do that.)

Finally, and seriously, as *Harvard Business Review*'s Amy Gallo says, "Focus on your perspective/observations to help them improve—not what you would do if you were boss."[15]

You deserve a little external help in your endeavors to rekindle inspiration. With a little well-informed effort on your part, you can put many of the surrounding dormant sources of inspiration to work, and put this Anti-Muse out of work.

11

The Bonfire

AARON COHN HAS built a human resources bot named Charlie.

I s#@! you not.

The founder of Happybot.ai has developed software intended to improve culture and happiness in the workplace by carrying out some of the morale-building activities often executed by an HR employee.

It automates activities like having an ice-cream cake show up on birthdays to remind employees they're cared for. It fuels camaraderie by organizing team dinners (including making reservations and collecting RSVPs) and sends managers daily self-development challenges to fuel personal growth. It conducts random acts of kindness like sending an employee a $10 gift card, just because, and collects feedback so employees feel heard. I'm not sure, but I think it can call you with an "emergency" in the middle of a meeting you desperately want to get out of. (If it doesn't do that, it should.)

It's an effort to scale some of the activities an HR person would do, things science says you should do, to help increase employee engagement and reduce turnover. This is important because, as Cohn told me, "Not every small company can afford a $100,000 HR person." It's an intriguing idea for big companies, too, as American Express is already piloting the bot.

My point in sharing this story is this: There is indeed a viable market for this artificial intelligence.

Why?

Because that's the state of the union.

Levels of disengagement are so high in the workplace, so many people have lost their sense of inspiration, that "robots" have arrived to help where an HR person isn't available or is overworked.

My fervent wish is that *Find the Fire* looks like major help for all of us on the front lines who are trying to rekindle our sense of inspiration. My hope is that it's a flamethrower we can use to strike back at nine mischievous fiends.

This chapter is about putting a hot, sharp edge to all the tools provided throughout this book so we can indeed fight back (side by side with Charlie if need be). As the bot provides organization and intention, so can this book if used to its full potential.

What follows is an organizing framework and quick-reference guide that puts all the fuel in one place to help you build a raging bonfire of inspiration.

The left column lists the nine Anti-Muses you might face, likely at different times and in varying degrees. Keeping this guide in front of you keeps you on high alert for each of the Anti-Muses (they tend to sneak back into action without giving you notice).

In the center column I list the antidotes to each Anti-Muse—a handy list of all the tools available within this book.

The column to the right lists antibodies, the specific resistances you will have built up by employing the antidotes (or tools) provided. Think of this column as the desired end states you're working toward sustaining over time—end states that negate each Anti-Muse.

TABLE 11-1

COUNTERING THE ANTI-MUSES

ANTI-MUSE	ANTIDOTE	ANTIBODY
Fear—Fear will never, ever stop if left unchecked. It holds us back and keeps inspiration from pressing us forward. It may be the most debilitating Anti-Muse of them all.	• "The Fear Effect" (the 5 ways fear assaults our sense of inspiration) • "The Fear of Failure Funnel" • "Frame of Mind" (6 ways to reframe how you think of failure) • "Frame of Reference" (7 ways to adjust our frame of reference to keep fear of failure from weighing us down) • "Frame of Action" (5 actions to take to beat back a fear of failure) • "9 Ways to Negate the Fear of Change" • "10 Ways to Overcome the Fear of Criticism"	An exhilarating freedom from a fear of failure, fear of change, and fear of criticism.
Settling and Boredom—When we're bored and have at the same time settled by not seeking out new challenges and experiences, we bypass a tremendous amount of potentially inspiring stimuli.	• "The Settling and Boredom Salvo" (4 self-promises to spring yourself out of stagnation) • "12 Tactics to Encourage Risk-Taking" • "Intent That Ignites" (4 powerful prompts to ignite your desire to get learning and growing again) • "Approaches That Accelerate" (4 ways to accelerate personal growth, including the "Goodness to Greatness Grid") • "The Window of Opportunity" (6 ways to make your own opportunities)	A continuous state of actively seeking out new experiences and opportunities for learning, growing, and success.

continued . . .

ANTI-MUSE	ANTIDOTE	ANTIBODY
Inundation—Feeling overwhelmed causes us to shut down and/or miss the cues of inspiration all around us. Survival mode replaces Inspired mode.	• "7 Methods to Help Make Choices and Prioritize" • "The Path Through Procrastination" (including "Up-Front Framing," "Future-You Fusion," "Getting Dialed-In," and "In-Process Excellence") • "6 Helpful Insults to Hurl at Your Inner Perfectionist" • "4 Ways to Push Back and Look Good Doing It" • "How to Ask for Help (HANDS)"	A sharp sense of progress, mastery, and preparedness along with the capacity to invite inspiration in.
Loss of Control—Working without a sense of control or autonomy, feeling disempowered, helpless, and checked out gives this Anti-Muse the control and sends inspiration packing.	• "The Flow of Power in Self-Empowerment" – "How You Give Away Your Power" (including 7 ways to break your people-pleasing habit, 6 steps to stop playing the victim, and the importance of overcoming negative self-dialogue) – "How You Can Take Back a Sense of Power" (including "The Power Grid—10 Self-Empowerment Tactics") – "How You Emit Power" (3 ways to do so, including "5 Crisis Control Lessons from 5 of America's Worst Crises")	A strong sense of empowerment and autonomy, feeling in control.

ANTI-MUSE	ANTIDOTE	ANTIBODY
Dwindling Self-Belief—When we begin doubting ourselves and can feel our confidence and inner resolve waning, inspiration doesn't stand a chance of being invited in.	• "11 Ways to Elevate Self-Confidence" • The ARC of Perseverance (including 3 truths to be aware of as you take on daunting challenges, 3 powerful ways to reframe your negative thought patterns in the midst of trying to persevere, and 5 ways to help you cope with the difficulties along the way) • "5 Musts for Being Mindfully Present" • 3-question framework to help you earn respect	An unwavering sense of self-confidence and perseverance, feeling respected and able to stay in the moment.
Disconnectedness—When we're disconnected from the people we spend so much time with at work, we deny ourselves the energy we could draw from such connections and thus snuff out a major source of potential inspiration.	• "The Chain of Camaraderie" – The Center Link (shared purpose, trust and truth, mutual respect) – Supporting Links ("9 Ways to Cultivate Camaraderie") – Repairing Weak Links ("9 Ways to Cultivate Healthy Debate", STEP BACK to harmonize with difficult coworkers)	A strong sense of camaraderie with your work compatriots.
Dearth of Creating—When we feel we've stopped creating and innovating, an unsettling sense arises that we're not using our abilities or generating meaningful and unique contributions. Inspiration we draw from our creations goes missing, and inspiration we draw on to create is absent.	• The STEM method for reigniting creativity (including 7 ways to introduce new stimulus into your life, 8 techniques for stimulating creativity, 4 factors for creating the right environment to spur creativity, and 5 mindsets that can foster creativity)	A feeling that your creativity is blossoming and that you're in the right state of mind and environment to be able to create.

continued . . .

ANTI-MUSE	ANTIDOTE	ANTIBODY
Insignificance—When we experience a feeling of insignificance, that what we're doing doesn't matter or make an impact, inspiration is doomed.	• 10 case studies on different ways to bring a greater sense of significance to your work	A feeling that what we do matters and that we are making a difference.
Lack of Evocation—When we work in conditions such that you can't imagine ever being inspired by anything, you're completely on your own to manufacture a sense of inspiration. A little external help can go a long way in the mission to reignite inspiration.	• "The Three Conditions of Evocation" • "The Three Behaviors of Evocation" (including "How to Morph Your Manager into a Source of Inspiration")	Feeling like you are part of an environment and conditions that you can be inspired by.

As a reminder, all of this can be leveraged not only to find inspiration in your current job once again, but also to keep your current job feeling inspiring (if you're so lucky that it feels that way already) or to inform your search for a new inspiring job (if you've decided that's necessary). It changes the questions you ask as you explore your new opportunity: "Is there a fear of failure rampant in this company?" "Do people seem absolutely inundated here?" "Do the people I talk to seem bored here?" "Do the people I meet feel their creative side is being tapped?" and so on. Signs that the nine Anti-Muses are largely absent means there's a good chance your sense of inspiration will stick in your new endeavor.

So there you have it—all the tools to reignite your own personal mission of becoming inspired at work once again.

You'll soon arrive at Destination Inspiration.

Let's make it a permanent stop, shall we?

ACKNOWLEDGMENTS

Let me start by acknowledging the acknowledgments section. It's like the safety instructions that airline cabin crew give—no one's listening other than those in the very closest rows—and even then, only out of obligation.

But that's OK because acknowledgments really aren't for all passengers. They're for those who have inspired and enabled the journey.

My most heartfelt thanks to the girls in my life—my daughter Emma, my wife Deb, my mom Dottie, and my sister Nancy. My two brothers Joe and Tim were just as important for inspiring this flight as well.

My thanks to the many people who shared their insights, stories, vulnerabilities, hopes, and aspirations with me along the way. Your input has enabled my output.

For readers sitting out of earshot of this attendant, you'll be landing shortly—in the state of the newly re-inspired.

NOTES

CHAPTER 1

1. K. Cavanagh, "The Shape of Things to Come: Inspiration in the Organizational Sciences," www.weatherhead.case.edu/departments/organizational-behavior/workingPapers/WP-14-02.pdf.
2. A. Potter, "Inspirational Leadership and Executive Presence: Research Findings," www.zircon-mc.co.uk(July, 2015).
3. Survey conducted among 1,100 executives across a range of companies varying in size from $1 million annual revenue to over $80 billion.
4. A. Linn, "Our Feeling About Work: Uninspired, Uncertain, and Not Very Optimistic," http://www.today.com/money/our-feeling-about-work-uninspired-uncertain-not-very-optimistic-6C9677701 (November 14, 2011).
5. E. E. Smith, "The Benefits of Optimism Are Real," https://www.theatlantic.com/health/archive/2013/03/the-benefits-of-optimism-are-real/273306/www.theatlantic.com (March 1, 2013).
6. J. H. Zenger. J. R. Folkman, and S. K. Edinger, *The Inspiring Leader*, New York: McGraw-Hill (2009), pp. 29–32.
7. Survey conducted among 1,100 executives across a range of companies varying in size from $1 million annual revenue to over $80 billion.
8. T. Thrash, A. Elliot, L. Maruskin, and S. Cassidy, "Inspiration and the Promotion of Well-Being: Tests of Causality and Mediation," *Journal of Personality and Social Psychology*, Vol. 98(3), 488–506 (March 2010).
9. L. Efron, "What to Do If You Are Disengaged at Your Job," https://www.forbes.com/sites/louisefron/2013/10/16/what-to-do-if-you-are-disengaged-in-your-job/#5fc114e17128 (October 16, 2013).
10. Thrash, Elliot, Maruskin, and Cassidy, "Inspiration and the Promotion of Well-Being."
11. Ibid.
12. T. Amabile and S. Kramer, "The Power of Small Wins," https://hbr.org/2011/05/the-power-of-small-wins (May 2011).
13. K. Cavanagh, "The Shape of Things to Come: Inspiration in the Organizational Sciences," www.weatherhead.case.edu/departments/organizational-behavior/workingPapers/WP-14-02.pdf.
14. S. B. Kaufman, "Why Inspiration Matters," https://hbr.org/2011/11/why-inspiration-matters (November 8, 2011).
15. T. Hart, "Inspiration as Knowing," in T. Hart, K. Puhakka, and P. Nelson, Eds., *Transpersonal Knowing: Exploring the Horizon of Consciousness*, Albany: State University of New York Press (2000).

CHAPTER 2

1. "The Legend of Cliff Young," www.elitefeet.com.
2. T. Jamieson, "Interview with Cliff Young," *New Vegetarian and Natural Health* (Winter 1997).
3. D. Hiskey, "A 61 Year Old Potato Farmer Once Won One of the World's Most Grueling Athletic Competitions," www.todayifoundout.com (October 27, 2011).
4. T. Hart, "Inspiration as Knowing" in T. Hart, K. Puhakka, and P. Nelson, Eds., *Transpersonal Knowing: Exploring the Horizon of Consciousness,* Albany: State University of New York Press (2000).
5. K. Cavanagh, "The Shape of Things to Come: Inspiration in the Organizational Sciences," www.weatherhead.case.edu/departments/ organizational-behavior/workingPapers/WP-14-02.pdf.
6. A. Read, "Taking the Plunge—How to Overcome Your Fear of Failure," www.lifehacker.com (August 12, 2015).
7. E. Gilbert, *Big Magic,* New York: Riverhead Books (2015), p. 26.
8. J. Goins, "You Need to Read The War of Art," www.goinswriter.com.
9. R. Jones, "What CEOs Are Afraid Of," www.hbr.org (February 24, 2015).
10. "Research Reveals Fear of Failure Has Us All Shaking in Our Boots This Halloween," www.marketwired.com (October 14, 2015).
11. C. Parker, "New Year's Resolutions That Connect with the 'Ideal Self' Are Most Effective, Stanford Psychologist Says," news.stanford.edu/2015/01/06/ resolutions-succeed-mcgonigal-010615/ (January 6, 2015).
12. Gilbert, *Big Magic,* p. 248.
13. "7 Ways to Overcome the Fear of Failure," www.pickthebrain.com/blog/ overcome-fear-of-failure/ (October 3, 2007).
14. "10 Ways to Overcome Your Fear of Failure," www.businesscollective. com/10-ways-overcome-fear-failure/.
15. P. Gardner, "Top 10 Success Stories of People Who Overcame Failure," www.careeraddict.com/top-10-success-stories-of-people-who-overcame-failure.
16. A. Sinclair, "Podcast 022: The Beginner's Guide to Overcoming Fear of Failure," https://allegrasinclair.com/overcoming-fear-of-failure/ (October 8, 2014).
17. Ibid.
18. Z. Hereford, "Overcoming Fear of Failure," www.essentiallifeskills.net/ overcoming-fear-of-failure.html.
19. B. Kane, "3 Proven Strategies to Help You Overcome Your Fear of Failure," blog.todoist.com/2015/04/14/overcome-fear-of-failure/ (April 14, 2015).
20. A. Read, "Taking the Plunge."
21. J. Hoover, "4 Tips to Help You Overcome the Fear of Failure," thejasonhoover.com/4-tips-help-overcome-fear-failure/ (May 8, 2015).
22. G. Winch, "10 Signs That You Might Have Fear of Failure," www. psychologytoday.com/blog/the-squeaky-wheel/201306/10-signs-you-might-have-fear-failure (June 18, 2013).

23. T. Knudson, "Why We All Have Fear of Failure," www.psychcentral.com/blog/archives/2014/06/23/why-we-all-have-fear-of-failure/ (June 23, 2014).

24. "Thomas J. Watson Quotes," www.brainyquotes.com.

25. Knudson, "Why We All Have Fear of Failure."

26. T. Lanier, "Fear of Failure: Why You Already Know How to Beat It," www.thenewmanpodcast.com.

27. N. Patel, "4 Ways to Deal with the Fear of Failure," www.inc.com (November 27, 2014).

28. Gilbert, *Big Magic*, p.254.

29. "Overcoming Fear," www.handbook-of-success.com.

30. D. Pros, "How to Overcome Fear of Failure like Apple's CEO Steve Jobs", www.dareandconquer.com/how-to-overcome-fear-of-failure-like-apples-ceo-steve-jobs/.

31. "7 Ways to Overcome the Fear of Failure."

32. E. Bridges, "The Top Reasons You're Not Overcoming Fear of Failure," www.finemortal.com/confidence/reasons-not-overcoming-fear-of-failure/.

33. T. Jamieson, "Interview with Cliff Young," New Vegetarian and Natural Health (Winter 1997).

34. V. Loder, "How to Conquer the Fear of Failure—5 Proven Strategies," www.forbes.com (October 30, 2014).

35. P. Ford, www.anxietybox.com.

36. H. G. Halvorson, "Explained: Why We Don't Like Change," www.huffingtonpost.com, (November 5, 2011).

37. A. Simon, "Why We're So Afraid of Change—And Why That Holds Businesses Back," www.forbes.com (April 8, 2013).

38. Ibid.

39. C. Scivicque, "Learning to Love Change in the Workplace," www.forbes.com (July 18, 2011).

40. www.goodreads.com.

41. B. Weston, "Love Change—10 Tips for Dealing with Change Positively," https://www.linkedin.com/pulse/10-tips-dealing-change-positively-your-workplace-ban-weston.

42. Parker, "New Year's Resolutions That Connect."

43. A. Dachis, "Why You're So Afraid of Change and What You Can Do About It," www.lifehacker.com/5982622/why-youre-so-afraid-of-change-and-what-you-can-do-about-it (February 11, 2013).

44. S. Goldberg, "The 10 Rules of Change," www.psychologytoday.com (September 1, 2002).

45. M. Borboa, "Get Over the Fear of Change and Change for the Better," www.sheknows.com/health-and-wellness/articles/805200/get-over-the-fear-of-change-and-change-your-life-for-the-better (August 8, 2008).

46. A. Williams, "What Makes a Critic Tick?" www.chicagoreader.com (July 4, 2002).

47. R. Baumeister, "Bad Is Stronger Than Good," *Review of General Psychology*, Vol. 5(4), 323–370 (2001).

48. www.goodreads.com.
49. M. Forleo, "4 Keys to Dealing with Criticism," www.youtube.com/watch?v=YwSU72bLEJc (July 9, 2013).
50. J. Clear, "Haters and Critics: How to Deal with People Judging You and Your Work," www.jamesclear.com/haters.
51. G. Parris, "Overcoming the Power of Criticism," www.ginaparris.com/overcoming_the_power_of_criticism/.
52. Clear, "Haters and Critics."

CHAPTER 3

1. L. Belkin, "Time Wasted? Perhaps It's Well Spent," www.nytimes.com (May 31, 2007).
2. T. Thrash, A. Elliot, L. Maruskin, and S. Cassidy, "Inspiration and the Promotion of Well-Being: Tests of Causality and Mediation," *Journal of Personality and Social Psychology*, Vol. 98(3), 488–506 (March 2010).
3. O. Burkeman, "This Column Will Change Your Life: Settling," theguardian.com (January 5, 2013).
4. "Creating a Risk-Taking Culture in a Risk-Averse Environment," www.greatworkplace.wordpress.com (April 14, 2010).
5. R. Ashkenas and L. Bodell, "The Reason Your Team Won't Take Risks," hbr.org/2014/09/the-reason-your-team-wont-take-risks (September 9, 2014).
6. S. Ismail, "3 Ways Companies Can Encourage Smart Risk Taking," www.entrepreneur.com (October 16, 2014).
7. D. McCarthy, "Turning Mistakes into Development," www.greatleadershipbydan.com (January, 27, 2008).
8. S. Shellenbarger, "What Makes a Risk Taker," www.wsj.com (May 22, 2013).
9. A. Sicinski, "How to Take Intelligent Risks in Pursuit of Your Goals," www.blog.iqmatrix.com.
10. B. Treasurer, "Safe Enough to Fail: How Leaders Can Encourage Risk-Taking and Innovation," www.td.org (October 16, 2014).
11. Ismail, "3 Ways Companies Can Encourage Smart Risk Taking."
12. Z. Sutton, "How to Beat Feeling Uninspired," fstoppers.com/originals/how-beat-feeling-uninspired-3973 (January 23, 2013).
13. J. Green, "Research Shows Nature Helps with Stress," dirt.asla.org/2011/09/08/research-shows-nature-helps-with-stress/ (September 8, 2011).
14. "Why You Should Stop Caring About Personal Growth," www.paidtoexist.com.
15. S. Young, "Why You're Exhausted but Not Improving," www.scotthyoung.com (August 15, 2011).
16. O. Kolodynska, "Overcome Frustration with These Inspirational Business Stories," www.livechatinc.com/blog/inspirational-business-stories/ (March 26, 2015).
17. R. Webber, "Make Your Own Luck," www.psychologytoday.com (May 1, 2010).

18. Ibid.
19. Ibid.

CHAPTER 4

1. S. B. Kaufman, "Why Inspiration Matters," www.hbr.org (Nov. 8, 2011).
2. T. Thrash, A. Elliot, L. Maruskin, and S. Cassidy, "Inspiration and the Promotion of Well-Being: Tests of Causality and Mediation," *Journal of Personality and Social Psychology*, Vol. 98(3), 488–506 (March 2010).
3. Towers Watson Global Workforce Study (2012).
4. J. Collingwood, "Hofstadter's Law and Realistic Planning," psychcentral.com/lib/hofstadters-law-and-realistic-planning/.
5. M. Dahl, "Don't Underestimate the Simple Power of Writing Down Your Goals," www.nymag.com (July 14, 2015).
6. N. Atik, "How to Stop Procrastinating," www.telegraph.co.uk (February 23, 2015).
7. R. Gonzalez, "Why Do We Work Better Under Pressure?" io9.gizmodo.com/why-do-we-work-better-under-pressure-1553149028 (April 11, 2014).
8. G. Ciotti, "The Science of Productivity," www.sparringmind.com/productivity-science/.
9. L. Nordgren, "The Power of Temptation," www.kellogg.northwestern.edu/news_articles/2009/nordgren_research.aspx (August 3, 2009).
10. E. Greenawald, "The Research-Backed Ways to (Finally!) Stop Procrastinating," www.themuse.com/advice/the-researchbacked-ways-to-finally-stop-procrastinating.
11. A. Swanson, "The Real Reasons You Procrastinate—and How to Stop," www.washingtonpost.com (April 27, 2016).
12. Ibid.
13. P. Stott, "How to Stop Procrastinating at Work," www.vault.com/blog/workplace-issues/how-to-stop-procrastinating-at-work/ (January 22, 2013).
14. Ciotti, "The Science of Productivity."
15. G. Ciotti, "How Our Brains Stop Us Achieving Our Goals and How to Fight Back," www.blog.bufferapp.com/how-our-brains-stop-us-achieving-our-goals-and-how-to-fight-back (July 11, 2012).
16. Ibid.
17. E. Jaffe, "Self-Imposed Deadlines Don't Stop Procrastination. Here's What Might," www.fastcodesign.com/3026895/self-imposed-deadlines-dont-stop-procrastination-heres-what-might (March 26, 2014).
18. P. Lavie, J. Zomer, and D. Gopher, "Ultradian Rhythms in Prolonged Human Performance," www.dtic.mil/get-tr-doc/pdf?AD=ADA296199 (February 1995).
19. J. Caldwell, "Sleep and Psychomotor Performance During Commercial Ultra-Long Range Flights," www.faa.gov.com (June 17, 2008).
20 www.pomodorotechnique.com.
21. B. Brown, "The Power of Vulnerability," www.ted.com/talks/brene_brown_on_vulnerability (June 2010).

22. C. Chua, "How to Overcome Perfectionism: Your Complete Guide," www.personalexcellence.co/blog/overcome-perfectionism/.

23. M. Twain, www.davesdailyquotes.com.

24. W. Baker, "5 Ways to Get Better at Asking for Help," www.hbr.org (December 18, 2014).

25. Y. Morieux, "How Too Many Rules at Work Keep You from Getting Things Done," www.ted.com/talks/yves_morieux_how_too_many_rules_at_work_keep_you_from_getting_things_done (July 2015).

26. A. Ayres-Deets, "How to Ask for Help (And Not Feel Bad About It)," www.thenextweb.com/lifehacks/2014/08/01/need-help-just-ask/#.tnw_WGXFsj5W (August 1, 2014).

27. S. Vozza, "How Leaders Can Ask for Help and Keep Their Team's Confidence," https://www.fastcompany.com/3047784/how-leaders-can-ask-for-help-and-keep-their-teams-confiden (June 25, 2015).

28. S. Roesler, "Help and How to Ask for It," www.allthingsworkplace.com/2009/06/we-all-need-help-managers-delegate-its-really-about-help-team-members-collaborate-and-it-would-be-great-if-our-kids-woul.html (June 5, 2009).

29. T. Watanabe, "Two Distinct Neural Mechanisms Underlying Indirect Reciprocity," *PNAS* Vol. 111(11), www.pnas.org (March 18, 2014), as cited in W. Baker, "5 Ways to Get Better at Asking for Help," www.hbr.org (December 18, 2014).

CHAPTER 5

1. P. Boffey, "Satisfaction on the Job: Autonomy Ranks First," www.nytimes.com (May 28, 1985).

2. M. Sirota, "People-Pleasing Always Backfires," www.huffingtonpost.ca (November 11, 2015).

3. "Bullying on the Job," www.abcnews.go.com, as cited in S. Biali, "How to Stop People-Pleasing," www.psychologytoday.com (October 11, 2013).

4. D. Bernstein, "Victim Mentality? Empowerment Through Self-Awareness," www.wakeup-world.com/victim-mentality-empowerment-through-self-awareness/ (December 8, 2015).

5. L. Becker-Phelps, "6 Signs of Victim Mentality," www.blogs.webmd.com/art-of-relationships/2016/05/6-signs-of-victim-mentality.html (May 18, 2016).

6. D. Neddermeyer, "Does Hypnosis Work? A Comparison Study," www.cuncecuncecunce.blogspot.com (September 13, 2006).

7. Survey conducted among 1,100 executives across a range of companies varying in size from $1 million annual revenue to over $80 billion.

8. M. Tyrrell, "Overcome Victim Mentality," www.uncommonhelp.me/articles/overcome-victim-mentality/.

9. Survey conducted among 1,100 executives across a range of companies varying in size from $1 million annual revenue to over $80 billion.

10. D. Schawbel, "Brene Brown: How Vulnerability Can Make Our Lives Better," www.forbes.com (April 21, 2013).

11. "Leadership Lessons We Learned on 9/11," www.coach4growth.com/leadership-skills/leadership-lessons-we-learned-on-911.

12. P. Sandman, "Anthrax, Bioterrorism, and Risk Communication: Guidelines for Action," www.psandman.com (December 29, 2001).

13. D. Wright, "Six Close Calls During the Cuban Missile Crisis," www.blog.ucsusa.org/david-wright/six-close-calls-during-the-cuban-missile-crisis-941 (October 30, 2015).

14. S. Berinato and T. Allen, "Leading Through a Major Crisis," www.hbr.org (October 2010).

15. Ibid.

16. Ibid.

CHAPTER 6

1. P. Kirch, "When Did the Polynesians Settle Hawai'i?" www.academia.edu/1034367/When_Did_the_Polynesians_Settle_Hawaii.

2. D. Carthage, "Stone Age GPS and the Discovery of Hawaii," www.pintsofhistory.com/2011/09/11/stone-age-gps-and-the-discovery-of-hawaii/ (September 11, 2011).

3. S. Bloom, "An Amazing Story of Determination That Will Inspire You to Take Action," www.dosomethingcool.net/amazing-story/ (September 6, 2013).

4. Carthage, "Stone Age GPS."

5. E. Ravenscraft, "Why Confidence Is So Important, and How to Improve Yours," www.lifehacker.com/how-to-build-your-confidence-and-why-it-matters-1442414831 (October 8, 2013).

6. Ibid.

7. Ibid.

8. T. A. Judge, E. A. Locke, and C. C. Durham, "The Dispositional Causes of Job Satisfaction," in L. L. Cummings and B. M. Staw (Eds.), *Research in Organizational Behavior*, Vol. 19, pp.151–188, Greenwich, CT: JAI Press (1997).

9. A. Phillips, "10 Ways for Women to Feel More Confident at Work," http://www.rawper.com/10-ways-women-feel-confident-work/.

10. K. Kay, C. Shipman, "The Confidence Gap," www.theatlantic.com (May 2014).

11. E. Roosevelt, www.brainyquotes.com.

12. L. K. Thaler and R. Koval, *Grit to Great*, New York: Crown Business (2015), p.60.

13. J. H. Zenger. J. R. Folkman, and S. K. Edinger, *The Inspiring Leader*, New York: McGraw-Hill (2009).

14. N. Burton, "The Secret of Self-Esteem," www.psychologytoday.com (November 20, 2014).

15. N. Branden, "What Self-Esteem Is and Is Not," www.nathanielbranden.com/what-self-esteem-is-and-is-not.

16. S. Cranston and S. Keller, "Increasing the Meaning Quotient of Work," *McKinsey Quarterly* (January 2013).

17. D. Diamond, "Just 8% of People Achieve Their New Year's Resolutions. Here's How They Do It," www.forbes.com (January 1, 2013).
18. R. Pasick, "Finding Strength in the Face of Adversity," www.robpasick. com/finding-strength-in-the-face-of-adversity/ (October 6, 2014).
19. A. Duckworth, "Grit: Perseverance and Passion for Long-Term Goals," *Journal of Personality and Social Psychology*, 2007, Vol. 92, No. 6, 1087-1101.
20. J. Clear, "The Science of Developing Mental Toughness in Your Health, Work, and Life," www.jamesclear.com/mental-toughness.
21. D. Querstret and M. Cropley, "Assessing Treatments Used to Reduce Rumination and/or Worry: A Systematic Review," *Clinical Psychology Review* (December 2013), Vol. 33(8), 996–1009.
22. J. Brownstein, "Planning 'Worry Time' Eases Anxiety," www.livescience. com/15233-planning-worry-time-ease-anxiety.html (July 26, 2011).
23. A. Chan, "9 Scientifically-Backed Ways to Stop Worrying," www. huffingtonpost.com, (October 1, 2013).
24. J. Polivy, C. P. Herman, and R. Deo, "Getting a Bigger Slice of the Pie. Effects on Eating and Emotion in Restrained and Unrestrained Eaters," *Appetite* (December 2010), Vol. 55(3), 426–430.
25. G. Ciotti, "How Our Brains Stop Us Achieving Our Goals and How to Fight Back," www.blog.bufferapp.com/how-our-brains-stop-us-achieving-our-goals-and-how-to-fight-back (July 11, 2012).
26. C. N. Trueman, "The Winter War," www.historylearningsite.co.uk/world-war-two/world-war-two-and-eastern-europe/the-winter-war-1939/the-war/ (May 14, 2015).
27. Ibid.
28. J. Clear, "Sisu: How to Develop Mental Toughness in the Face of Adversity," www.jamesclear.com/sisu-mental-toughness.
29. "The Humongous Difference Between Persistence and Perseverance and How One Is Ruining Your Life," www.alifeonyourterms.com/persistence-and-perseverance/.
30. C. Bergland, "The Neuroscience of Perseverance," www.psychologytoday. com (December 26, 2011).
31. Ibid.
32. S. Bradt, "A Wandering Mind Not a Happy Mind," www.news.harvard. edu/gazette/story/2010/11/wandering-mind-not-a-happy-mind/ (November 11, 2010).
33. H. Reeder, "3 Steps to Boosting Your Charisma," www.psychologytoday. com (August 26, 2014).
34. J. Grabmeier, "Multitasking May Hurt Your Performance, But It Makes You Feel Better," www.researchnews.OSU.edu/news/2012/04/30/ multitask/ (April 30, 2012).
35. M. Formica, "5 Steps for Being Present," www.psychologytoday.com (June 14, 2011).
36. J. Hamilton, "Think You're Multitasking? Think Again," www.npr.org (October 2, 2008).
37. S. Weinschenk, "The True Cost of Multi-Tasking," www.psychologytoday. com (September 18, 2012).

38. A. Gorlick, "Media Multitaskers Pay Mental Price, Stanford Study Shows," www.news.stanford.edu/2009/08/24/multitask-research-study-082409/ (August 24, 2009).

39. J. Kleiman, "How Multitasking Hurts Your Brain (and Your Effectiveness at Work)," www.forbes.com (January 15, 2013).

40. S. Weinschenk, "Why We're All Addicted to Texts, Twitter and Google," www.psychologytoday.com (Sept. 11, 2012).

41. A. Flores, "Be Present at Work," http://www.foxnews.com/lifestyle/2012/05/16/aurelia-flores-be-present-at-work.html (May 16, 2012).

42. Formica, "5 Steps for Being Present."

43. J. Dixit, "The Art of Now: Six Steps for Living in the Moment," www.psychologytoday.com (November 1, 2008).

CHAPTER 7

1. H. Huhman, "The Hidden Benefits of Happy Co-Workers," www.entrepreneur.com/article/238122 (October 8, 2014).

2. L. Bigelow, "How to Improve on Building Authentic Relationships in the Workplace," www.smallbusiness.chron.com/improve-building-authentic-relationships-workplace-19153.html.

3. C. Gregoire, "Why You Should Care About Having Friends at Work," www.huffingtonpost.com (July 9, 2013).

4. L. Petrecca, "At Best Places to Work, Trust, Pride and Camaraderie Overshadow Pay," USAToday.com (October 28, 2011).

5. J. Smith, "How Much Coworker Socializing Is Good for Your Career?" www.forbes.com (September 24, 2013).

6. A. Hall, "The Key to Happiness at Work That Has Nothing to Do with Your Actual Job," www.huffingtonpost.com (February 24, 2015).

7. J. Shriar, "How Coworkers Affect Your Job Satisfaction," www.officevibe.com/blog/how-coworkers-affect-job-satisfaction (August 5, 2015).

8. C. Riordan, "We All Need Friends at Work," www.hbr.org (July 3, 2013).

9. M. Ingold, "Why Mutual Respect in the Workplace Should Be HR's Main Focus," www.benetechadvantage.com/why-mutual-respect-in-the-workplace-should-be-hrs-main-focus (August 20, 2015).

10. A. Grant, "Friends at Work? Not So Much," www.nytimes.com (September 4, 2015).

11. Ibid.

12. Huhman, "The Hidden Benefits of Happy Co-Workers."

13. "The Importance of Connecting with Colleagues," www.bloomberg.com (June 10, 2010).

14. Ibid.

15. S. Marsar, "Camaraderie in the Firehouse," www.firerescuemagazine.com (February 10, 2013).

16. D. Burkus, "Why Fighting for Our Ideas Makes Them Better," www.99U.com/articles/7224/why-fighting-for-our-ideas-makes-them-better.

17. Ibid.

18. L. Dishman, "How to Disagree With Your CEO and Not Get Fired," www.fastcompany.com (June 4, 2014).
19. G. Patton, www.brainyquotes.com.
20. Burkus, "Why Fighting for Our Ideas Makes Them Better."
21. "Workplace Conflict and How Businesses Can Harness It to Thrive," *Global Human Capital Report*, www.cpp.com (July 2008).
22. D. Berenbaum, "Six Strategies for Dealing with Difficult People," http://www.communicoltd.com/Resources/Articles/Customer-Service-Communication-Coaching-Skills/Six-Strategies-for-Dealing-with-Difficult-People.aspx.
23. T. English, "5 Tips for Dealing with Difficult Co-workers," https://www.linkedin.com/pulse/5-tips-dealing-difficult-co-workers-thrive15-tim-english (September 15, 2015).
24. Ibid.
25. "Workplace Conflict and How Businesses Can Harness It to Thrive."
26. S. Collins, "Work It Out: Getting Along with Co-Workers," www.webmd.com/balance/features/getting-along-with-coworkers#1 (August 10, 2012).
27. M. McKee, "The 5 Manners of Dealing with Difficult People," www.mannersmentor.com/only-at-work/how-to-deal-with-difficult-people.

CHAPTER 8

1. T. Thrash and A. Elliot, "Inspiration as a Psychological Construct," *Journal of Personality and Social Psychology*, Vol. 84(4), 871–889 (2003).
2. B. Josephson, "Unleash Your Creativity (It's Up to You)," huffingtonpost.com (October 14, 2014).
3. B. Tracy, "Success Newsletter," (August 25, 2016).
4. A. Kleon, *Steal Like an Artist*, New York: Workman Publishing (2012).
5. Ibid.
6. J. James, "Be Our Guest: Unleashing Creativity & Innovation," www.inc.com (January 8, 2014).
7. T. Seelig, "The Science of Creativity," www.fastcompany.com (April 17, 2012).
8. S. B. Kaufman, "Why Inspiration Matters," www.hbr.org (November 8, 2011).
9. S. Shellenbarger, "Better Ideas Through Failure," www.wsj.com (September 27, 2011).
10. D. Burkus, "3 Ways Leaders Accidentally Undermine Their Teams' Creativity," www.hbr.org (July 7, 2015).
11. S. B. Kaufman, "The Emotions That Make Us More Creative," www.hbr.org (August 12, 2015).
12. L. Widrich, "Why We Have Our Best Ideas in the Shower: The Science of Creativity," www.blog.bufferapp.com/why-we-have-our-best-ideas-in-the-shower-the-science-of-creativity (February 28, 2013).
13. M. Wilson, "4 Myths About Apple Design from an Ex-Apple Designer," www.fastcodesign.com/3030923/4-myths-about-apple-design-from-an-ex-apple-designer (May 22, 2014).

14. L. Gratton and T. Erickson, "Eight Ways to Build Collaborative Teams," www.hbr.org (November, 2007).
15. Ibid.
16. D. Domeyer, "Your Guide to Building the Best Creative Team," www.roberthalf.com/creativegroup/blog/your-guide-to-building-the-best-creative-team (May 17, 2016).
17. J. Kotecki, *Penguins Can't Fly*, New York: St. Martin's Griffin (2015).
18. L. Hill, G. Brandeau, E. Truelove, and K. Lineback, "The Inescapable Paradox of Managing Creativity," www.hbr.org (December 12, 2014).
19. Ibid.
20. Ibid.

CHAPTER 9

1. S. B. Kaufman, "Why Inspiration Matters," www.hbr.org (November 8, 2011).
2. G. A. Saedi, "E.M.P.O.W.E.R. Yourself Today," www.psychologytoday.com (January 8, 2012).
3. C. Bates, "Global Celebrity Culture Is Fuelling Our Crippling 'Fear of Insignificance,' Warns Psychologist," www.dailymail.co.uk (February 15, 2011).
4. Towers Watson Global Workforce Study (2012).
5. J. Williams, "Nora Ephron, the Queen of Quips," www.artsbeat.blogs.nytimes.com (June 27, 2012).
6. C. McGrath, "Nora Ephron Dies at 71; Writer and Filmmaker with a Genius for Humor," www.nytimes.com (June 27, 2012).
7. A. Levy, "Nora Ephron Knows What to Do," www.newyorker.com (July 6, 2009).
8. F. Rich, "Nora's Secret," www.nymag.com.
9. McGrath, "Nora Ephron Dies at 71."
10. C. Nickisch, E. Bernstein, and J. Bunch, "The Zappos Holacracy Experiment," www.hbr.org (July 28, 2016).
11. J. Reingold, "How a Radical Shift Left Zappos Reeling," www.fortune.com (March 4, 2016).
12. Ibid.
13. B. Mycoskie, "How I Did It: The TOMS Story," www.entrepreneur.com (September 20, 2011).
14. Ibid.
15. J. Quittner, "What the Founder of TOMS Shoes Is Doing Now," www.fortune.com (September 8, 2016).
16. "Blake Mycoskie's Bio," www.toms.com.
17. L. Najafi, "Usain Bolt's Net Worth as He Goes for More Gold in 2016 Olympics," www.gobankingrates.com/personal-finance/usain-bolt-net-worth-gold-2016-olympics/ (August 12, 2016).
18. "Usain Bolt Insists to Shoot All Advertisements in Jamaica to Give Back to His Community," www.firstpost.com (July 21, 2016).
19. A. Vagianos, "Inspiring Campaign Highlights the Power of Women Helping Women," www.huffingtonpost.com (June 23, 2016).

20. S. Sandberg, "Together Women Can: Celebrating the Power of Women Helping Women," www.huffingtonpost.com (June 23, 2016).

CHAPTER 10

1. Give Kids the World, www.gktw.org.
2. I. Smith, "The Disruption Model of Inspiration: Toward a General Model of 'Being Inspired to Act,'" collections.lib.utah.edu/details?id=196721 (August 2014).
3. C. Fader, "Fact Check: Teacher Makes Dramatic Point About Military Service," www.jacksonville.com/news/metro/2010-12-12/story/fact-check-teacher-makes-dramatic-point-about-military-service (December 12, 2010).
4. K. Cavanagh, "The Shape of Things to Come: Inspiration in the Organizational Sciences," www.weatherhead.case.edu/departments/organizational-behavior/workingPapers/WP-14-02.pdf.
5. T. Thrash, A. Elliot, L. Maruskin, and S. Cassidy, "Inspiration and the Promotion of Well-Being: Tests of Causality and Mediation," *Journal of Personality and Social Psychology*, Vol. 98(3), 488–506 (March 2010).
6. Towers Watson Global Workforce Study (2012).
7. "Study Reveals That Bad Boss Can Make Employees Sick," www.apost.com/en/blog/study-reveals-that-a-bad-boss-can-make-employees-sick/440/.
8. R. Madell, "Snarky Coworker Got You Down?" www.careerintelligence.com/work-with-people-you-dont-like/ (February 5, 2015).
9. "No. 1 Reason People Quit Their Jobs," www.webcenters.netscape.compuserve.com/whatsnew/package.jsp?name=fte/quitjobs/quitjobs.
10. Ibid.
11. J. Zenger, J. Folkman, and S. Edinger, *The Inspiring Leader*, New York: McGraw-Hill (2009).
12. Conclusions from an independent survey of 3,000 managers.
13. Ibid.
14. K. Dill, "5 Things You Can Do to Improve Your Relationship with Your Boss (and Your Next Boss)," www.forbes.com (October 17, 2014).
15. A. Gallo, "How to Give Your Boss Feedback," www.hbr.org (March 24, 2010).

INDEX

Printed in the USA
CPSIA information can be obtained
at www.ICGtesting.com
JSHW082319140224
57417JS00002B/15